How to
Evangelize
And the
Art of
Preaching
(English Edition)

How to
Evangelize
And the
Art of
Preaching
(English Edition)

MARTIN LIONEL LUBIN

ARPress
ILLUMINATING IDEAS
EMPOWERING VOICES

ARPress
45 Dan Road Suite 5
Canton MA 02021
Hotline: 1(888) 821-0229
Fax: 1(508) 545-7580

Ordering Information:
Quantity sales. Special discounts are available on quantity purchases by corporations, associations, and others. For details, contact the publisher at the address above.

Printed in the United States of America.

ISBN-13:	Softcover	979-8-89676-043-6
	eBook	979-8-89676-044-3

Library of Congress Control Number: 2024927271

Table of Contents

PREFACE

Let the cross shine, and may its rays penetrate the corners and recesses of all the continents! The blessed hope must shine from kings' palaces to poor men's cottages, from the pinnacle of the learned to the barbarian's hut. The call of the man of Calvary will resound in hearts, and finally, on the great day of eternity, we shall see them come from east and west, the children of the Lord redeemed by His grace, glorified by His presence: men and women, black and white, free and slave, small and great, rich, and poor, clothed in holiness seated with the heralds of faith in God's eternal kingdom. Then the Lord's dream will be fulfilled since the good news of the kingdom will have been preached throughout the world, and each will have their testimony (Matthew 24:14).

All this will happen because of these men, these valiant servants of God who knew how to respond to their Master's call to service. Passionate for Him, and carried away by their sense of duty, they have traversed the world, spreading everywhere along their path the good seed of the Gospel, and finally the earth will have been filled with the knowledge of God, just as the waters cover the sea bed (Hab. 2:14).

The history of the Church keeps the imprint of these men, and will forever remain engraved with their hard work. Whether through the transcription of the Bible verse by verse by the Waldensians of Piedmont in France and its translation into English by Wycliffe, as a sacred legacy made to his people; whether through the protesting cries of the Reformers such as John Huss preaching obedience to God's Word, Martin Luther proclaiming salvation by grace, Calvin preaching spiritual growth, the Anabaptists reclaiming baptism by immersion, Wesley proclaiming holiness, Miller announcing the return of Jesus, and the Seventh-day Adventist movement reintegrating Sabbath observance into Protestant worship, the proclamation of the Gospel will have made its way through the ages, and will resound even more strongly in these difficult days, the last of world history announcing nothing but the hecatomb of the human race.

But according to prophetic revelation, the greatest spiritual revival that has ever taken place on the face of the globe must take place, well before the total collapse of our world. Already barriers tending to oppose the proclamation of the Gospel are falling day by day so that the way may be cleared before the messengers of salvation in their work as conquerors for Christ. And the more we advance, the more we also witness the return of apostolic days whether by pen or by voice until the final triumph of the proclamation of the Gospel.

Therefore, this book is written in the perspective of this great and final spiritual revival. Convinced of the imminence of this day, and living already in this moment, the author of this work, Martin Lionel Lubin, my longtime friend, has chosen to offer his readers a course of action, a repertoire of information, a sure reference, as lovers of Christ and His message, in fulfilling the imperative demand of the Apostle Paul which is to "preach the Word" 2 Timothy 4:2.

This work, I dare confess, is the product of a life dedicated to Evangelism and the edification of the Church. Without having been officially called as a pastor at the level of the worldwide Church, Martin Lionel Lubin, yet a true pastor at the local Church level, has entrusted to these pages the task of communicating to his readers this flame that has burned in his soul since his encounter with Christ.

After having been watered at the source of the living waters of salvation, and after having led many thirsty souls to quench their thirst at this same source, some of whom are today ministers of the Word; Elder Martin Lionel Lubin wants to disclose it, share it, what shall I say inject it into all of us, so that we too might do the same.

From then on, we hold these pages not as mere theory, but as a powerful testimony of a servant of God to catalyze, train, and engage other men and women in spreading the good news of Jesus Christ whether personally or publicly.

I am persuaded that the reader with penetrating insight, and eyes trained to see the invisible, will find through these pages hidden jewels that will fill them with joy and happiness. I remain convinced that this book is a call to reflection, to questioning, to meditation and prayer for all who will venture into penetrating its lines; and I pray that far from remaining buried, the pearls gathered from this reading will in turn be exposed to the contemplation of our family members, our neighbors and our friends in general, so that finally, more terrifying than the roar of the lion, may resound to the ends of the world, the cry: Jesus is coming!

Dr. Yrvain Jean-Philippe

Pastor of the Seventh-day Adventist Church

APPRECIATION

In this book entitled "HOW TO EVANGELIZE AND THE ART OF PREACHING", Martin Lionel Lubin provides essential and even indispensable elements that can contribute to the training of all those who passionately engage in evangelization and preaching of the Gospel of Jesus Christ.

He seeks to initiate his audience to preach with Bible texts, not about the Bible. This is why he presents in his book the notion of homiletics and exegesis. In this end-time generation, God's people need such a tool to revive the flame of Bible study, evangelization, and preaching. It is undoubtedly a work that invites us to engage in the divine mission.

Vaillant Youte

Pastor and Director of Personal Ministries and Sabbath School at the Quebec Conference of Seventh-day Adventists.

ACKNOWLEDGMENTS AND DEDICATIONS

I want to express, here, my feelings of deep gratitude to all those who, from near or far, have accompanied me in this endeavor of publishing this work. I want to name specifically:

- Dr. Yrvain Jean-Philippe, Senior Pastor of the Horeb Adventist Church of New York.

- Dr. Robert Jean-Marie Charles, Coordinator of Franco-Haitian Ministries at the Greater New York Conference.

- Vaillant Youte, Pastor and Director of Personal Ministries & Sabbath School at the Quebec Conference of Seventh-day Adventists.

- Joseph Dély, Pastor For their availability, advice, and suggestions.

I also dedicate this work:

- To my family members:
- My wife: Suzette.
- My children: Sandra, Greggy, Givens.
- My son of heart, Robert, for whom I have great consideration.
- To the members of Temple I Adventist Church of Port-au-Prince, to which I remain very attached during fifty-two (52) years of my journey within the Seventh-day Adventist Church, and which has been for me a fertile source of inspiration.
- To my Colleagues of the Pastoral Body of this Church who have always shown and still show me all their consideration and fraternal affection.

- To all young people, but a youth that is not necessarily defined by age, but rather by the dimensions of heart and spirit
- Finally, to all those, Christians of all stripes, Men and Women, who, although living in a world in disarray and moral decay, still dare to speak of hope and who nurture in their hearts and minds, the taste for eternal realities.

Martin Lionel Lubin

FOREWORD

The title of this work submitted to the reader's attention: **"How to Evangelize and the Art of Preaching"**, refers to two (2) essential concepts of Christian life: **Evangelization and Preaching.** They find their foundation and justification, on one hand, in Jesus' great evangelical commission: "*Go, make disciples of all nations*", Mat. 28:19 and Paul's exhortation to Timothy: "*Preach the word, be prepared in season and out of season; reprove, rebuke, exhort, with complete patience and teaching*" 2 Tim 4:2.

This work is addressed first to all those who want to get involved in evangelical activities, such as neophytes and young people, and to all those who already make preaching their daily concern. For the latter, this will be a platform for recycling and refreshment.

We have taken care to develop notions such as missionary visits and Bible study, considered as gateways to evangelical activity.

Evangelizing is a complex task that requires implementing a whole series of techniques. Evangelization is increasingly asserting itself as a science that, if it wants to achieve its objectives, must necessarily draw from modern human sciences: psychology, sociology, pedagogy, etc. This is no longer the time when one can act blindly. Anyone who ventures to participate in evangelization without preparation takes a risk, although the conversion of a soul depends primarily on the action of the Holy Spirit. People may, in good faith, want to be useful to the Lord's cause; but if they are not trained or coached in this direction, they will never be able to do worthwhile work. More than ever, church members in general, and young people in particular must be interested in participating in missionary training programs where techniques for conducting a missionary visit, Bible study, and different ways of being useful to the community in humanitarian and social activities are taught.

Knowledge and deepening of God's Word must be the primary objectives of all those who want to prepare for eternity. Consequently, a special chapter is devoted to a series of Bible studies. The originality of the presentation of this series, focused on explanations and comments relating to the themes treated, makes it possible for it to be easily exploited, autonomously, either by inexperienced preachers or by readers who do not have the accompaniment of monitors. Mastery of basic biblical doctrines cannot be achieved with less effort.

Regarding preaching, we have not considered and covered all aspects of a field as vast as homiletics, which is taught over several sessions in universities or theological Seminaries. We have dealt with, relative to homiletics, notions that we believe to be essential and indispensable.

Certainly, we have set ourselves a challenge: that of developing, in a single work, two (2) themes of extreme importance: Evangelization, Preaching, and a teaching framework: a Series of Bible studies. Each of these fields could have, by itself, been the subject of a separate work, with an exhaustive deepening of the field considered. But we have rather chosen to give the reader an overview of these three fields at once; this choice is voluntary.

Our main objective is to present the essential elements of these fields that can facilitate understanding for all those who are already interested in them or who are thinking of getting involved in the future. In a word, conciseness has been our goal.

Having said this, the field remains open to all those who want to deepen their knowledge in these areas and make more advanced pointed studies; moreover, fortunately, we live in the age of virtual and digital libraries where, with just one click, we have at our disposal almost all the authors of the world.

Finally, to the extent that the content of this book can be an important auxiliary for all those interested in evangelization and preaching, the objective set by the author will have been largely achieved and all glory is to God.

CHAPTER 1 - WHAT IS PREACHING?

The very content of this work suggests, at the outset, not only a clear definition of the concepts of preaching, Homiletics, and Evangelization but also an understanding of the links or relationships existing between them.

Let us start by asking ourselves this question: What is preaching?

A first definition leads us to say this: "To preach is to communicate the Word of God, most appropriately, to provoke a transformation in the life and heart of those who hear it"

From this definition emerge three (3) main components of preaching:

- The fact of preaching the Word
- The most appropriate way to present it
- The objective of preaching

1. Preaching the Word:

Patrice Vivarès declares: *"God speaks to us today when we reread this text (of the Bible). The preacher must raise himself from the text: we do not preach about the Bible but from the Bible to proclaim the Good News of the risen Christ today." "In preaching, we do not have to tell our personal story, but to attest to God's story in our life."*

This truth is well confirmed by the Apostle Paul who declares: *"For there is one God and one mediator between God and mankind, the man Christ Jesus, who gave himself as a ransom for all people. This has now been witnessed at the proper time. And for this purpose, I was appointed a preacher and an apostle—I am telling the truth, I am not lying—and a true and faithful teacher of the Gentiles." 1 Timothy 2:5-7*

"And of this gospel, I was appointed a preacher and an apostle and a teacher." 2 Timothy 1:11

According to Paul, the preacher is established to instruct. Therefore, the purpose of preaching is to instruct and train. Preaching must not be the product of human reflection but must have the Bible as its main source. He must not preach about the Bible but from Bible texts. Paul says: "Now to him who can establish you following my gospel, the message I proclaim about Jesus Christ, in keeping with the revelation of the mystery hidden for long ages past, but now revealed and made known through the prophetic writings by the command of the eternal God so that all nations might believe and obey him" Romans 16:25-26.

According to this text, preaching must be done according to revelation according to the word of God (Colossians 1:25-27). From this text, we discern the requirement that is imposed on one who wants to be a preacher.

2. The Most Appropriate Way:

This refers well to the methods to use and ways to communicate the Word. It must be remembered that there are several ways to transmit the message, depending on the personality of the preacher and the environment in which he operates. There is no method that is, from the start, superior to another; but you must choose the most appropriate one.

A preacher will succeed by adopting one style or way of communication, whereas another might fail. However, one must always be inspired by the classical methods proposed by Homiletics; that is to say, there is a technical aspect of preaching that must be considered.

3. Achieving the Purpose of Preaching: Transformation

The primary goal of preaching is salvation, which is achieved by provoking transformation in hearts. This distinctly differentiates a preacher from an ordinary speaker.

The latter primarily addresses the intellect of their audience. Their success is often measured by how well they persuade or impress through solid and well-documented arguments. The preacher, on the other hand, speaks primarily to the heart and soul of their audience.

This does not mean the preacher neglects or ignores a methodical approach to their sermons. On the contrary, they must remain a lifelong student of the Bible, open to all significant scientific developments and international issues, to stay relevant. However, their primary objective is not to showcase knowledge or expertise but to reach and transform souls.

In the New Testament, the Greek word used for preaching is *"kerygma,"* derived from the verb *"kerysso,"* meaning "to proclaim a message, to herald." Thus, *"kerygma"* translates to "proclamation, message, preaching." The person delivering the message is the preacher or herald (*"keryx"*).

Alfred Kuen summarizes: *"To preach is to exercise authority and announce, in God's name, the demands and promises of Holy Scripture as expressions of God's will—expressions that commit us. A preacher cannot merely inform; they must also inspire, communicate new visions, and establish spiritual goals. Preaching is motivating—giving listeners a reason to commit their entire lives to the faith of the Gospel."*

The Importance of Preaching

Preaching is the main course or the centerpiece of any spiritual program, whether it is a worship service or an evangelistic meeting. The preaching of God's Word is indispensable to God's people. It represents God's proclamation to the congregation of believers and the world. Through preaching, people hear about God and come to faith in Him. Preaching leads the world to find God.

In Romans 10:14-15, the Apostle Paul says: *"How, then, can they call on the one they have not believed in? And how can they believe in the one whom they have not heard? And how can they hear without someone preaching to them? And how can anyone preach unless they are sent?"*

This text emphasizes that faith is birthed through preaching. A preacher is a laborer in the Word of God. Bernard Reymond asserts: *"Christianity should no longer be considered, particularly by its adherents and especially by preachers, as a religion of the book, but as a religion of the 'living word'—a word that circulates, surprises, sometimes eludes, and is always there to be heard rather than merely read."*

To fully grasp the value of preaching, consider conducting a small survey among a group of visitors to a particular church. Ask each of them: *"What impressed you most and led you to return repeatedly to this congregation?"* You might be surprised to learn that preaching is their primary point of interest.

However, it is important to note that preaching is a double-edged sword, as it can both attract and diminish interest depending on the messenger and the quality of the message. The same message delivered by three different preachers or evangelists will yield three different results or impacts. These variations depend not only on the personality of the preachers but also on the methods they employ. This leads one Christian author to declare that preaching can be the expression of the best or the worst.

Is Preaching in Crisis?

Preaching should be the essence of worship, providing spiritual nourishment for God's people. Yet, it often occupies a diminished role in worship services.

Bernard Reymond describes the crisis facing worship and preaching: *"Churchgoers, whether frequent or occasional, have noticed this shift in their ministers' attitudes: While sermons in the early 20th century could last close to an hour or more, by the 1950s, they were often reduced to twenty minutes, then fifteen, and by the 1980s, they sometimes occupied less than ten minutes. Regardless of whether attempts to renew worship succeed or fail, the issue of preaching and the lack of enthusiasm for it remains. For instance, some pastors see no problem in expanding other elements of liturgy—lengthening prayers, for example—while simultaneously reducing the time and importance of the sermon."* (De Vive Voix, p. 17, Editions Labor et Fides, 1998)

Preaching: A Science or an Art?

To answer whether preaching is a science or an art, consider the following experiment: Enroll three students in the same theology program, where they study homiletics under the same professors and have access to the same library for four years. At the end of their studies, you might find three different levels of preaching—ranging from mediocre to excellent.

This suggests that theoretical knowledge gained in a university or seminary is insufficient to make someone an effective preacher. The individual's personality plays a critical role. In other words, beyond technique or science, personal talent or natural gift—whether innate or developed through experience and practice—must also come into play. In summary, preaching is both a science and an art; however, it is more art than science.

Experience demonstrates that these two components—science and art—do not contribute equally to the preacher's profile. The preacher's natural talent and personal aptitude predominantly determine their effectiveness in preaching. Thus, while preaching involves elements of science, it is largely an art.

The Elder and Preaching

Who is an elder? An elder holds the highest position within the hierarchy of the local church. They serve as the church leader—a pastor, but at the local level, with their jurisdiction limited to the congregation that appointed them. Another defining characteristic of an elder is volunteerism; they are not paid for their work and are not administratively accountable to higher church authorities. This volunteer aspect highlights the nobility of their role.

As a pastor, an elder's primary responsibilities are preaching and teaching—feeding the people of God. The Apostle Peter describes this role: *"To the elders among you, I appeal as a fellow elder and a witness of Christ's sufferings who also will share in the glory to be revealed: Be shepherds of God's flock that is under your care, watching over them—not because you must, but because you are willing, as God wants you to be; not pursuing dishonest gain, but eager to serve."* (1 Peter 5:1-2)

Since preaching is the elder's main function, they should spare no effort in improving their abilities to fulfill this duty effectively. This includes being a fervent student of God's Word and taking advantage of every opportunity to receive training in the art of preaching. However, this effort requires a key quality: humility—the ability to self-examine and recognize one's weaknesses. Patrice Vivarès notes: *"Preaching is a school of humility. We must relinquish our own words and remain selfless, not seeking to please men (especially if influential figures are present). We learn patience as we come to terms with our imperfections, and courage in risking disapproval. Preaching demands continuous intellectual labor and spiritual exercise."* (*L'Appel de la Parole*, p. 62)

While an elder's primary responsibility is preaching, it is not their sole duty. They are also a leader, chosen partly for their leadership abilities. The Apostle Paul tells Timothy: *"The elders who direct the affairs of the church well are worthy of double honor, especially those whose work is preaching and teaching."* (1 Timothy 5:17)

In this passage, the Greek verb *"proïstēmi"* (from *pro*, "before," and *histēmi*, "to stand") translates as "to lead, manage, govern, direct, or preside." Paul teaches Timothy that elders are leaders and administrators. Among them, some are dedicated to preaching and teaching.

An elder may not be an exceptional preacher but can still be a good leader—a person who blesses the church through their ability to guide, counsel, and provide spiritual care. Preaching is a gift, and not everyone is endowed with it, even those who make preaching their daily focus or ministry. However, the art of preaching can also be learned through practice and experience.

A Christian community should never exclude someone from the role of elder solely because they are not an outstanding preacher, especially if they are a capable spiritual leader. The role of an elder encompasses various aspects, with preaching being only one part.

CHAPTER 2 - THE MESSENGER: THE TEN (10) QUALITIES OF THE PREACHER

While recognizing that this list is not exhaustive, we will indicate here ten (10) qualities that we believe to be essential for a preacher.

1. Piety

Piety is the first quality of a preacher. If the goal of preaching is to provoke a change or transformation in a person's life, to bring them closer to Jesus; how can we want to bring someone closer to Jesus if we do not first care about approaching Him personally? This leads us to speak of "evangelism", a concept that could mean "living the Gospel we preach".

"God wants the one who teaches the Bible to be, in his home, a demonstration of the truths he proclaims. A man's life has more influence than his words. Daily lived piety will give the preacher's testimony great strength. Patience, the agreement of theory and practice, love finally will make an impression on hearts that sermons cannot exercise" **(Ellen G White, Gospel Ministry, p.199)**

2. Sincerity

Sincerety can well be defined as an agreement between what one does and what one says.

"To be sincere is to live by one's convictions and words, it is not to have two lives, one public and one private, different from each other. The word sincere comes from the Latin "sine cere" which means: without wax; without makeup, without a mask. To be sincere is to have nothing to hide" **(A. kuen, How to Preach or the Art of Communicating the Essential p,37)**

Spurgeon, speaking of a Pastor whose life did not correspond to what he preached said: *"he preached so well and lived so badly that when he was in the pulpit, everyone said he should never come down from it, and when he was out of the pulpit, all declared that he should never go back up to it,"* **A. Kuen, How to Preach or the Art of Communicating the Essential, p. 36**

3. Humility:

The preacher should always strive to efface himself to let Christ's glory be seen through his messages. Pride is the greatest professional danger for the preacher. The successes we record in our preaching career, the compliments received and the marks of consideration expressed towards us can make us spiritual "monsters", without even realizing it. Receive these marks of attention with the greatest humility and glorify God for it.

4. Courage:

Preaching sometimes arouses misunderstanding, opposition, and bitterness; the preacher should be forewarned and face it with courage and determination. The Bible teems with examples, in both the Old and New Testament, where the spokespersons of the Lord had to face serious difficulties in executing their missions. This should encourage us and strengthen our faith in our tasks as preachers. Perseverance and endurance must be our essential mark. The prophets of Baal, as well as Jezebel, opposed the prophet, Elijah; Jeremiah experienced opposition, and Micah likewise.

John the Baptist paid for his courage with his head for having denounced Herod's adultery.

5. Tact:

While it is true that the preacher must preach the truth, it is also true that he must do so with tact. Truth must not be spoken in just any way. This is where all the preacher's talents related to psychology and sociology must come into play.

"In the work of winning souls, great tact and wisdom are necessary. The Savior never concealed the truth, but He always spoke it with love. In His dealings with others, He showed the greatest tact, and He was always

kind and thoughtful. He was never rude, never needlessly spoke a severe word, never gave needless pain to a sensitive soul. He did not censure human weakness. He fearlessly denounced hypocrisy, unbelief, and iniquity, but tears were in His voice when He uttered His scathing rebukes. He never made truth cruel, but always manifested deep tenderness for humanity."
(Ellen G. White, Gospel Workers, p. 117)

6. Conviction and Persuasion:

One who is not convinced himself cannot convince others. If the message is presented with softness, indifference, and nonchalance, it will be received with a corresponding effect by the listeners. The preacher must be persuasive and speak with conviction. During message preparation, the preacher should strive, alone, to simulate its delivery, not only to measure its duration but also body language (gestures), force, and style of presentation.

7. Attention to External Presentation:

The preacher must watch over his clothing and language:

- Clothing must be dignified, clean, and without eccentricity.
- Good diction, voice must be clear, and distinct.
- Language must be simple, natural, friendly, and never vulgar.

8. Optimism:

The preacher must be positive in thinking about success. On one hand, he must remember that his success does not depend on his talents and abilities. The techniques learned and practiced in the context of preaching cannot help convince a soul of sin and bring it to give itself to God. On the other hand, one must avoid measuring the success of preaching by the immediate visible response given by the audience the number of souls who physically manifest to accept the Lord or to reconsecrate themselves. It happens that the seed of the Gospel thrown into hearts does not produce immediate fruits, but does a subtle and slow work that will be manifested long after. The conversion of a soul does not depend on us; we only throw the seed of the Gospel. Let us not take God's place.

9. **Message Preparation:**

The preacher must prepare his message; and take the time to gather all information, documents, and files that correspond to the subject he proposes to deal with. He can prepare a sermon that, although personal, is inspired by an article that seems to reflect the truth he wants to state. Cobbling together and combining a few verses, up until a few hours before presenting before an audience, is not preaching, or is doing it very clumsily. Negligence and carelessness are the most serious faults of a preacher. Presenting oneself before an audience to speak in the name of the Highest is the greatest honor that can be given to a mortal; to do it without preparation is to dishonor God.

10. **Adaptation: Message-Audience**

The preacher must adapt his message to his audience. Audiences are often diverse, depending on the intellectual and social level of the majority. The preacher must be understood so that his message can be grasped. Before an audience is made up of people of humble condition, never use words that might give the impression that you have learned. Preach in the manner of Jesus. His messages of love were adapted to his audience. He knew how to say a word at the right time to one who was in sadness. In a word, the preacher should always adapt his style, language, and illustrations to the level of those who listen to him

CHAPTER 3 - HOMILETICS: DEFINITION AND CONTENT

The word "**homiletics**" comes from the Greek "**homilia**" which means: conversation, discourse, or speech. This said, oral communication is at the very heart of homiletics; but a very special communication, turned towards the Word of God. But, if one wants to effectively communicate the Word of God, there are rules related to communication that it is necessary to learn, to know, to respect. In a word, homiletics can be defined as: "the learning of the art of preaching"

It is from the word "**homiletics**" that comes "**homily**". The homily is a sermon, a conversation, a dialogue, a discourse, and a speech. The art of giving a sermon is homiletics. But homiletics is not preaching, it is a technique that allows a preacher to communicate his preaching. According to Bernard Reymond, "Homiletics is not strictly speaking preaching; it is a reflection on preaching. If the homily is a form of preaching, homiletics is the theological discipline that has this preaching as its object."

Homiletics is the theological discipline that deals with the transmission of the word.

Homiletics is the art of preaching God's word with power. A preacher's task consists of making the message of God's word penetrate the minds of listeners so that it transforms their lives. Homiletics allows the preacher to properly use the text of God's word in his preaching. It helps the preacher produce an edifying, constructive, and solid sermon. When preaching, the text of God's word must not be used as a springboard. One must speak from the text. Patrice Vivarès says: "The preacher must raise himself from the text; we do not preach about the Bible but from the Bible to proclaim the Good News of the risen Christ today."

Homiletics is a theological reflection on God's word. It must consider present reality. Theology is a discourse about God that must call upon the practice of the environment. In the context of homiletics, a theological discourse is preaching.

Homiletics is the means used to transmit the word. In good preaching, there must be teaching that pushes a person to act in both the short term and long term. The preacher must go looking in his preaching for the public while respecting the biblical text. He must not use biblical texts to express his ideas or to blame. But he must let himself be guided by the Holy Spirit to share God's word with believers. Moreover, preaching must be a sharing. It must provoke dialogue. This is why a preacher needs to master homiletics well to give life to preaching.

CHAPTER 4 – EVANGELIZATION: TOOL OF SALVATION

- **Evangelization**

The word "Evangelization" comes from "gospel", itself derived from Greek (Evangelion), which means "good news". Evangelization is the act of announcing the Gospel, "the good news" of Jesus Christ, thus making known the Christian faith. In a word, to evangelize is to proclaim the good news.

The word **"evangelization"** does not appear in the Bible. But the words "evangelize" and "evangelist" are used in the New Testament. The verb "evangelize" from the Greek "euangelidzo" is used 52 times in the New Testament. This verb comes from two Greek words: "eu" which means "well, good" and "anangello" which means **to report, communicate news, a message**. Therefore, the Greek verb "euangelidzo" means to announce good news, a message concerning Jesus Christ.

Evangelization is a message centered on Jesus. The apostles like Andrew, Philip, and Paul have left us good examples (see John 1:40-51; 1 Co 2:1-5). The word "evangelist" is used three times (see Acts 21:8; Eph 4:11; 2 Ti 4:5). The evangelist brings the message of Jesus Christ to the world. In 2 Timothy 4, verse 5, the Apostle Paul says to Timothy: "But you, be sober in all things, endure hardship, do the work of an evangelist, fulfill your ministry."

- **Evangelization: an imperative**

Evangelization must be a priority in the life of the Christian who acts as a disciple of Jesus Christ. He must intend to evangelize in everything he does. In other words, he must intentionally serve the surrounding community to lead all those who are interested in the Word of God to Christ.

In his exhortation to Timothy, the apostle Paul asks to do the work of an evangelist. To do the work of evangelization is to accomplish an action. According to Paul, an evangelist's work consists of accomplishing an action.

Ellen G. White declares: *"When the Church shall have ceased to deserve the reproach of indolence and laziness, the Spirit will be manifested. Divine power will be revealed. The children of God will see the dispensations of the Lord of hosts. Divine light will project its beneficial rays, and, as in the time of the apostles. Many souls will abandon error to turn to truth. The earth will be lit with the glory of God. I was shown that God's people expect a change to occur, that a compelling power takes hold of it. But we will be disappointed in this expectation, we must act, we must get to work, and earnestly ask God to give us an exact knowledge of ourselves. The scenes unfolding before us are impressive enough to incite us to awaken and communicate the truth to all who would hear it. The harvest of the world is about to ripen."*

- ## The content of evangelization

Evangelization is the proclamation of the good news of salvation to bring thirsty souls for truth to Christ.

We distinguish two (2) types or methods of evangelization: personal evangelization and public evangelization.

Evangelization is personal or individual when it is carried out in a "soul to soul" or "person to person" approach. Bible study is the perfect type of personal evangelization. Evangelical practice has demonstrated the full value of this type of evangelization; because it allows for familiar dialogue and a closer relationship between the preacher (teacher) and the student who can better express their concerns and questions regarding spiritual matters. Many souls that we encounter each day will never be brought to the knowledge of truth if they are not personally approached.

Deacon Philip's contact with the Ethiopian Eunuch is a perfect illustration (Acts 8:34,35). Jesus, during His earthly ministry, found Himself on several occasions in one-on-one encounters with souls.

Evangelization is public when the objective is to reach many people at once. This type of evangelization which is more complex requires a whole organizational setup. It must be planned and nothing should be neglected or left to chance. It is an unforgivable mistake to start an evangelical campaign without adequate sufficient preparation. This preparation takes time; but there is no classical time or duration applicable to all cases and in all regions or geographical spaces. This time will vary according to:

    a. The scope of the program and the number of people available for its execution.

    b. The community's experience with these types of programs

    c. The duration it must cover.

- **The organization or planning of public evangelization**

Without being exhaustive or limiting, the following elements or points should be included in any public evangelization program:

1. The period or duration of the program
2. The choice of speaker or preacher
3. The theme of the campaign
4. The choice of a steering committee, including different cells or personalities:

    a. One (1) Coordinator, with one or two Deputy Coordinators (as the case may be)

    b. A Secretariat

    c. A Treasurer

    d. A visitation cell

    e. A prayer cell

    f. A logistics cell

    g. A musical cell

    h. A protocol cell

    i. A platform cell

    j.   The Church Pastor (ex officio member)

- **The functioning of the steering committee**

In the context of the steering committee's operation, we must highlight here the roles and responsibilities of the different units:

1. The steering committee groups the different units or cells' plans and defines the general orientation of the campaign. It meets periodically before and during the execution of the campaign. Its decisions are made by consensus or with the majority vote, but never according to the unilateral wish of the coordinator.

   The coordinator is not necessarily the Personal Ministries leader the one who oversees directing the community's evangelical activities. However, when the Personal Ministries leader is not chosen as Campaign Coordinator, it is customary that they be one of the Deputy Coordinators.

2. The person responsible for each cell, who is a member of the committee, is assisted by other members in executing the tasks assigned to this unit; this constitutes a sub-committee.

3. The Secretariat is responsible for recording visitors, statistics, and minutes of meetings.

4. The Treasurer, within the framework of the voted budget allocated to the program, receives funds from the church board and voluntary donors. Expenses are made with supporting documents; a periodic financial report is submitted to the steering committee and a final financial report to the church board at the end of the campaign.

5. The visitation cell plans visits before and during the campaign; certainly, with the participation of all church members.

6. The prayer cell coordinates a prayer program before or during the execution of the sessions.

7. The logistics cell is responsible for everything related to electricity, air conditioning, heating, audio (sound), videography, computer technology, and transportation.

8. The musical cell plans: a. The rotation of musical groups and artists b. The rotation of organists and other instrumentalists c. The musical program of the sessions and fills in for absences, if necessary

9. The protocol cell follows visitors, from their entry into the meeting room until the end of the sessions.

10. The platform cell plans the rotation of those sitting at different sessions.

11. The above scheme proposed for the organization and functioning of the steering committee is not absolute. It represents a frame of reference that can be modified and adapted according to circumstances and needs. That said, the number of units planned can be decreased or increased, depending on available human resources and the scope of the evangelical program.

12. A cell leader, within this committee, should be chosen based on their known and proven sense of responsibility. People known to be negligent should be excluded. Because the cell leader must be the first to ensure the proper functioning of their unit if we want the system to work well globally. For example:

13. The Music Leader should always make it their duty to make, from the day before, a telephone reminder or text message to all persons (artists, musicians, groups) scheduled for the execution of a point at the day's session; and if there is a failure, take urgent measures to fill the gaps.

14. The Logistics Leader should, each day, take measures to correct or repair any problem posed the day before relating to logistics (Audio-visual, air conditioning, heating, electricity, etc.)

15. The Platform Leader should make sure, through a reminder, that all people scheduled to execute a point tomorrow are well reached or warned.

Also, it must be remembered that the coordinator of the steering committee is not a simple convener called to chair meetings. They have an active role: that of permanently coordinating the activities of the different cells. However, they should not directly interfere in the tasks assigned to these different units, nor replace the holder. Their role is to ensure that everyone does their work at the right time. To do otherwise would be to get involved in too many activities at once, become exhausted, and result in ineffective management of this committee.

- **Digital evangelization**

The reality of COVID-19 has disrupted and changed the style of life at the global community level. Strong concentrations of crowds are discouraged and even individual meetings between people become almost impossible if one wants to consider the social distancing advocated by political leaders. This also constitutes a major challenge for Christian religious communities accustomed to provoking large gatherings of people. This challenge obliges world spiritual leaders to innovate in a new type or new method of evangelization that can be called "digital or virtual evangelization."

This method intends to utilize all available internet and computer resources for the benefit of evangelization. This means using, the internet, mobile phones, and social media platforms (Facebook, YouTube, Zoom) to reach thousands of people across the world. It means using radio and television to transmit the message.

However, it must be recognized that digital evangelization remains a palliative or shortcut that never has the same impact as public evangelization.

This method of evangelization has both advantages and disadvantages.

The main advantage of digital evangelization is the fact of reaching several thousand people at once, spread across different geographical spaces and distant from the broadcast center. In this sense, it satisfies the objective of public evangelization which intends to reach many people at once.

The other advantage is that this system does not require a sophisticated institutional setup, as highlighted in the case of the steering committee in relation to public evangelization. The only main character remains the preacher and very few human resources are mobilized.

The great disadvantage of this method is the absence of interactions or direct communication with the people reached by the program. These people are not even known or identified. As such, no follow-up of interested persons can be done, either during or after the evangelical activity. This is so true that when convinced souls want to make a decision, they are automatically directed to the closest religious communities for support.

The other disadvantage is that virtual evangelization may require relatively high operating costs when referring to expenses necessitated by the acquisition, maintenance, and operation of related equipment. For example: the cost of internet subscription access, purchase of cameras, microphones, headphones; cost of spaces on online platforms (zoom), etc.

To this must be added the availability of qualified human resources to manage the system and the fees to be granted to them, if one must pay for the corresponding services. Consequently, it is advised that communities who want to set up such a system choose a special team to manage it. The latter is headed by a coordinator, assisted by other people having expertise and experience in the field of audio-visual, computer science and online broadcasting. The people chosen to integrate this unit should be chosen based on their high sense of responsibility and their availability.

Given the operating costs inherent to digital evangelization or any other form of online broadcasting, the local church committee should be willing to allocate an appropriate share of its budget to this project. In case the budgetary possibilities of this community cannot cope with it, they should solicit special donations from members or a one-time grant from the Mission, Federation, or Conference that oversees them.

- **Relationships or links between Evangelization, Preaching and Homiletics**

Evangelization and Preaching: They both have in common the communication of God's Word. Evangelization aims exclusively to communicate this Word to an audience not yet initiated into the science of salvation, by proclaiming the good news to them, thus bringing them to accept the Christian faith. On the other hand, preaching, for its part, aims not only at this category of listeners but also at those who are already connected to the Gospel. Under this latter aspect, preaching therefore also aims to consolidate faith, edify, and strengthen those who have already met Jesus once in their life. That said, preaching is broader and more encompassing than evangelization. Preaching addresses all categories of listeners.

Homiletics: For its part, homiletics, by proposing to develop techniques in the art of preaching, therefore has a common point with both evangelization and preaching. It provides both with the necessary materials for their effectiveness.

CHAPTER 5 - THE MISSIONARY VISIT

The missionary visit is the first step in personal evangelization; it is moreover the simplest step for those who want to be initiated into evangelization.

5.1 Its Importance

There is nothing that can replace the value of personal and individual contact. This method is suggested to us by the Savior himself who, on many occasions, was face-to-face with souls thirsting for love, knowledge, and salvation. We saw him face-to-face with Nicodemus; we saw him face-to-face with the Samaritan woman. The pressures of modern life, professional activities, and attachment to training leave very little time for certain people to decide, by themselves, without external invitation, to participate in a religious program.

Yet sincere souls are thirsting for truth in this category, just waiting for an invitation to be extended. These people will never be in contact with the Gospel if no one enters their house or their office. Those who, as servants of God, show indifference to missionary visits unknowingly close the door of salvation to many sincere souls. Many of these souls are ready to respond to our invitation; they are only waiting for our visit because the Spirit of God has already prepared them accordingly. *"Many are on the threshold of the kingdom of heaven, only waiting for the invitation to enter"* **Ellen G. White, Evangelism, p. 265**

Ellen G. White suggests methods that can be used to evangelize. She speaks of personal work as a method. This personal work is house-to-house work. She says: "House-to-house work is as important as public conferences. In large cities, certain classes of society will not come to meetings. We must look for them as the Good Shepherd looks for the lost sheep. Serious personal effort must therefore be made in this direction."

She adds: "Preaching the message in big cities is not enough, we must also work the soil of the field; we must do house-to-house work... The truth must not only be exposed during meetings; house-to-house work must be accomplished."

5.2 Different Forms of Missionary Visits:

Several methods or approaches can be used in the context of evangelical work carried out through missionary visits. There is not a method that is superior to another. In each case, one must choose the one that best suits:

1. The objective that has been set
2. The categories of people who will be visited
3. The profile of the individual visiting (intellectual abilities, doctrinal knowledge, etc.)

In the context of this work, four (4) methods have been retained; but they are not limiting, as others have also been tested.

5.2.1 Invitations to Meetings or Biblical Conferences:

In general, the level of attendance or success of a series of biblical conferences depends largely on the level of promotion and awareness that is made of it. Certainly, it must be recognized that, nowadays, the development of the internet and social media (Facebook, WhatsApp, Instagram) can play a determining role, as vectors of communication in invitations to be launched, either to a wide audience or to targeted people. However, in communities or regions with weak or non-existent computer infrastructure, one can launch direct invitations, and use cards or leaflets to distribute to neighbors, friends, relatives, or acquaintances.

5.2.2 Systematic Monthly Distribution of Religious Newspapers:

In the context of this method, these newspapers are offered each month (for a certain number of months) to people we want to reach with the Gospel and with whom it is difficult to make contact otherwise. We can cite for example Ministers, General Directors, Doctors, Professors, Lawyers, State Officials, Politicians, etc.

Enriching experiences have been recorded by church members in the context of the distribution of newspapers such as Sentinel, Signs of the Times, Priorities, etc.

5.2.3 Distribution of Printed Materials

This method involves identifying or preparing a series of Bible studies presented in printed form and distributing them periodically to people targeted in advance. The effectiveness of this method lies in the regularity of distribution and the logical sequence of subjects presented, according to a pre-established sequence, for example, subject #4 cannot be distributed before subject #3, nor #10 before #9,

This method requires rigorous planning and an appropriate budget. When using this method, one should never give interested persons the impression that the printed materials are worthless. For this, at the distribution of each new number, it would be wise to ask the person their impressions or questions about the previous number.

5.2.4 Invitation to Social Programs

It is especially at this level that we must present the social and humanitarian side of the Gospel. People living in the communities we want to evangelize are sensitive to the interest we take in their health, education, professional life, etc. in a word their practical life. This is moreover Jesus' message and method: to be interested in the whole person, in their totality. The people to whom we are called to present the message of salvation will be more receptive to this word if they feel that we are first interested in them.

Show an active love to the people we encounter. In this context, one can decide to launch invitations to programs or seminars relating to:

- Preventive health
- First aid
- Childcare
- Home arts
- Cutting and sewing
- Literacy etc.

Ellen G. White says: "Christ's method alone will give true success in reaching the people. The Savior mingled with men as one who desired their good. He showed His sympathy for them, ministered to their needs, and won their confidence. Then He bade them, 'Follow Me.'"

This is how, through personal effort, one must establish a close relationship with people. Better results would be achieved if less time were spent preaching and more time visiting families.

Evangelism as Prescribed by the Bible is not rooted in a method. It is something more. In His method, Jesus asked people to follow Him by presenting them with the message of salvation. Ellen G. White never reduced evangelism to a method. She emphasized that:

"The medical missionary opens the door to the Gospel. It is as much through his art as through preaching that it must be proclaimed. Everywhere, there are people to whom the Word of God has never been presented and who do not attend any religious service. For the Gospel to reach them, it is necessary to find them at home. Relieving their suffering often provides a means of approach. Missionary nurses who provide care in families or visit the poor encounter many opportunities to pray, read passages of Scripture, and talk about the Savior." — **Ellen G. White, *Ministry of Healing*, p. 118**

5.3 Visiting Techniques

A missionary visit is, by nature, simple and can be practiced by everyone, even beginners taking their first steps in evangelism. However, certain techniques should be learned to make visits more effective. The four techniques presented here are as follows:

5.3.1 Two by Two

Experience and practice recommend that a missionary visit should not be carried out alone. It is advisable to operate "two by two," and it is even preferable that the participants be of opposite genders. The presence of individuals of opposite genders can greatly facilitate understanding and connection between the parties, regardless of the gender of the person being visited. Furthermore, the "two by two" technique aligns with the method employed by Jesus.

"Then He called the twelve, and began to send them out two by two, giving them authority over unclean spirits."— Mark 6:7

"After this, the Lord appointed seventy-two others and sent them two by two ahead of Him to every town and place where He was about to go." — Luke 10:1

This means that no one went alone; a friend was paired with a friend and a brother with a brother. This allowed them to seek each other's counsel, encourage one another, and pray together.

5.3.2 How to Introduce Yourself

Although it may seem simple, the way one presents themselves at the door or the apartment of the person being visited requires following and respecting certain rules.

1. Presentation

At the door, knock respectfully, that is, with gentle knocks—not too loud. If there is a doorbell, ring it, but do so intermittently; do not press and hold the button for too long. Such missteps could disturb the person and create a negative disposition toward you.

2. Greetings

When the door opens, greet the person kindly. Avoid a stern or sullen expression. Apologize for disturbing them or for taking up their time.

3. Stating the Purpose of the Visit

When explaining the purpose of your visit, be convincing, persuasive, and engaging. Never give the impression that you are there to ask for something or request a favor. Instead, give the impression that you have come to offer something. Your first words are very important. Introduce your companion and give a concise and clear explanation of the purpose of the visit. There is no single style of presentation that applies to all cases; it varies depending on whether it's an invitation to a Bible conference, the distribution of printed materials or religious journals, or invitations to social programs.

5.3.3 Duration of the Missionary Visit

The missionary visit should be brief. Once the purpose has been stated, bring the visit to a close and leave. Avoid unnecessary small talk. Do not waste the valuable time that your host has given you, or you risk not being welcomed back. Avoid bringing up subjects or personal questions that could embarrass the person.

5.3.4 Your External Appearance During the Visit

Do not forget that external appearance greatly influences the impression you make on the person receiving you. Avoid a sloppy appearance. Dress in your best clothes; they should be clean, and your shoes well-polished. As the adage says, "Clothes do not make the man, but they allow him to be recognized." Through your external appearance, show your host that you represent the King of kings.

CHAPTER 6 - THE MESSAGE: CLASSIFICATION OF BIBLICAL MESSAGES

Biblical messages are classified according to two (2) major criteria:

    a. About recipients those who are called to receive the message.

- Bible study
- Lay preaching
- The sermon

    b. About content and the constituent elements of the message:

- Topical or thematic sermon
- Textual or expository sermon
- Narrative sermon

I BIBLE STUDY

1.1 Bible Study: Why?

After the missionary visit, Bible study is the most direct form of personal evangelization from soul to soul. The large crowd concentrations recorded during these last forty (40) years in the context of public evangelization can never replace the benefit of personal contact, with an open heart, with a soul.

We are called to follow Jesus' example every day. He takes a personal interest in the concerns of each soul in search of truth and love. His contact with the Samaritan woman not only regenerated her but through her, many people living in Samaria. "Come, see a man who told me everything I ever did. Could this be the Christ?" Luke 4:29. "And many more believed because of His word." Luke 4:41

The Ethiopian eunuch was penetrated by the message of grace and baptized, thanks to the ministry of Deacon Philip who, in personal contact, explained passages of God's Word to him. It is a wonderful and extraordinary work that church members enter homes, open the Bible, and communicate the message of salvation to thirsty souls.

"Christ's work was largely made in one-on-one conversations. He attached great value to conversations he could have with just one soul, and this single soul transmitted to thousands of others the teachings received." Ellen White, Evangelism, p. 59

Ellen White affirms that *the method of work through Bible studies is divinely inspired.* She also emphasized the importance of the small home group method. For her, "The formation of small groups to carry out evangelical action is a plan that was shown to me by Him who cannot make mistakes. If the Church is numerous, let the members be distributed in small teams to work not only for the faithful but also for unbelievers".

The accomplishment of this task requires appropriate training of those who must be involved in it. Young people and adults who want to be effective in Bible study work should take more interest in missionary training seminars when these are organized. Interested readers will find in this work the necessary ingredients to be effective in evangelization in general, and the practice of Bible study in particular.

This is what Ellen G. White indicates in her work "Evangelism": "A well-conducted work will have excellent results in cities where a Bible course can be organized to train instructors while public conferences are being held. Experienced servants of God possessing a deep spiritual sense should give their advice daily to Bible instructors."

1.2 Bible Study, What Is It?

Bible study can be defined as the study of the Holy Scriptures through questions and answers. One should avoid giving Bible study the appearance of a sermon or speech where only one person speaks and an audience listens attentively. Bible study must take the form of a conversation, although exchanges with the executor must be made according to well-determined order and rules. Every lay preacher should expect that participants' questions will indicate the degree of receptivity or assimilation of the theme treated at the end of a Bible study presentation. The preacher's objective should be, not to preach, but to instruct.

1.3 The Organization of a Bible Study

The identification of the student is the starting point of a series of Bible studies. The interested person is perhaps spotted through missionary outings; perhaps a friend, a neighbor, a classmate, an office colleague, etc., in a word, a person willing to receive Bible study:

- The systematic distribution of printed pages and religious newspapers offers an excellent means to establish contacts with individuals and propose Bible studies to them.

- The colportage of religious books and those dealing with health and scientific subjects opens the way for colporteurs to identify potential Bible students. In this case, these people's interest is already awakened to spiritual subjects.

- Radio and television broadcasts sponsored by evangelical sectors can be excellent means to launch invitations to Bible studies.

- Humanitarian, health, and social programs where there is a strong concentration of people can offer a special opportunity to make invitations to a Bible study program.

1.4 The Periodicity of Study

Once the Bible student has been identified, the lay preacher must agree with them on a set of points, namely: How many times per week or month will the course be given? Which days? At what time? etc. None of these decisions should be made unilaterally. This is to respect the programs and use of time of all parties.

1.5 Planning the Study Series

This involves answering a set of important questions: that is, how many subjects will the series include? What subjects will be covered and in what order?

The subjects retained will depend on the duration of the series. The shorter the series, the more doctrinally consistent the subjects must be; because essential biblical doctrines must be presented there.

Whatever the number of subjects planned, the strong point of planning a series of Bible studies is the order of subjects that corresponds to a logical sequence, going from the simplest to the most complex. The preacher should never make the mistake of dealing with subjects at the beginning of the series that should be dealt with in the middle or at the end; this would be giving solid food to a baby.

1.6 Development of Teaching Tools

Just as a worker must equip himself before starting work, the preacher must ensure the availability of necessary teaching tools. Besides the accessories he may have at his disposal such as books, religious newspapers, etc., the main materials required are:

1. Bible Study Manual

No Bible study manual can be privileged over others because each gives details that perhaps others do not present. In this sense, the preacher can glean from several manuals at once to prepare a subject. Bible pouches are not recommended for beginning lay preachers, because they do not offer explanations and comments often so indispensable to mastering certain questions.

2. A Bible

There are several versions of the Bible, but it is recommended that the preacher's Bible be the version most used in the region; for example: the Louis Second version, for French-speaking areas; and the King James version, for English-speaking ones.

1.7 Subject Preparation

This is a point of capital importance: subject preparation. The preacher should give it all his attention; he must meticulously prepare each subject before presenting himself to the Bible class.

1.8 Execution of Bible Study

1.8.1 Number of students in the study

If, in general, a study is conducted with a single student, there is nothing wrong with the audience being composed of several people; this is even recommended because it's throwing the seed of the Gospel into several hearts at once. However, when the preacher is inexperienced, his best audience should be one person.

1.8.2 The preacher's arrival

When arriving at the place where the study is to be held, first establish friendly and courteous contact with those present. Show the interest you take in the family. If someone is absent, note it. Never show that you have come to execute a mission in a dry and mechanical way. Be gentle.

1.8.3 The progress of the study

1. **Prayer**

   A short prayer should begin the study; it can be made either by the preacher himself or by his companion, if there is one. In some cases, you can even invite one of the students to pray, if there is a disposition to do so. But here, be careful, and avoid embarrassing people.

2. **The introduction**

   If this is not the first subject of the series, make a brief reminder of the last subject treated. The introduction, as in all cases, has the objective of making general considerations to make the connection with the theme to be studied. However, avoid making this introduction too long, thus making precious time indispensable to the development of the study.

3. **The development of the study refers to the following points:**

   a. **Questions and texts:**

   There is no ideal number of questions to consider for building a study subject; it depends on the nature of the subjects and the time allocated to each session. More consistent doctrinal subjects may require a greater number of questions and texts than others. In all cases, care must be taken that the verses cited correspond well to the appropriate answer to the questions.

   It is recommended to have the Bible students themselves read the texts; however, to facilitate their task, you should first identify the corresponding page number for the verses to be read, or help them find the passages. However, if you are visibly in the presence of participants who cannot or do not want to read change methods. Avoid embarrassing or disturbing people.

   b. **Explanations and comments:**

   The explanations and comments relating to the texts read constitute the basis of the study. This is where the preacher conveys his message. Each text of each question aims at the overall understanding of the theme under study. The explanations given should be clear and easily assimilable.

c. The recapitulation:

At the end of the presentation, briefly recall the main points of the study to fix them in the minds of your interlocutors.

d. Student questions:

If Bible study is a dialogue, it is especially here that this dialogue is engaged, through participants' questions. These questions are very important because they allow the preacher to measure the impact of his presentation. However, they should always be encouraged to ask questions only related to the theme studied. If a question relates to a subject that will be dealt with later in the series, it must be postponed with gentleness and courtesy. If a general question is asked that is not planned in the study curriculum, the preacher should arrange a special appointment with the students to answer their concerns.

e. Final prayer:

A short prayer ends the study; it is made either by the preacher or by his companion.

1.9 Duration of Study

There is no classic duration to propose for a study session, it varies according to the availability of the student and the preacher; but experience has shown that a duration of thirty (30) minutes is ideal for the presentation of the subject, outside of student questions.

1.10 General Advice

Relating to Bible Study: a. Avoid presenting several subjects at once. b. Present the Word of God, avoiding condemning others' religious beliefs. c. Respect the study duration agreed with the student. d. Be attentive to student questions. e. Do not include in your study difficult-to-understand texts that might better suit an advanced Bible class.

II – LAY PREACHING

Lay preaching is the biblical message addressing an external audience not yet initiated into the Gospel. This message which is mainly doctrinal aims to lead the listener to accept and practice the truths that are taught to them. The second form of biblical message, lay preaching is the perfect type of public evangelization or evangelization targeting several people at once. Lay preaching is speaking to crowds; This enters the very practice of Jesus and the Apostles. On the day of Pentecost Peter spoke to a crowd, and that same day three thousand (3,000) people were converted and baptized (Acts 2:41).

However, if public evangelization presents certain advantages, it must in no way prevent or diminish the value of individual contact with souls. That said, a whole organization must be put in place by the evangelical team to meet visitors individually. These meetings should have, among other objectives, to:

- Show visitors appreciation for their presence and interest in the programs.
- Answer their questions and concerns.
- Consolidate undecided souls.

Unlike Bible study, characterized by dialogue and simplicity, lay preaching is a religious service involving many more points and diversities. Here, contact with the audience is not as personal, nor as familiar as in Bible study.

1. Message Preparation

Even more than Bible study, lay preaching requires rigorous and careful preparation. More elaborate documentation must be made available to the preacher; this includes files and articles related to the theme to be treated. The preacher should also ensure the availability of appropriate audio-visual support if these should be necessary during the presentation before the audience.

Unlike Bible study, a written plan is needed so that ideas can be expressed in an orderly way. It is an unforgivable fault for a preacher to present himself before an audience without a plan or written guide. This written plan should include an introduction, different parts or sections of development, and a conclusion.

In the introduction, a few brief minutes should be arranged to a) make the connection between the last subject presented and the one announced. b) prepare listeners' minds for understanding the message to be presented.

Development constitutes the main dish of the message; its duration will depend on the nature of the subject and the overall time allocated to the program. Some subjects may require a more elaborate presentation than others, but this does not authorize the preacher not to circumscribe his message within a well-determined duration; otherwise, he would end up losing the audience's attention during his presentation and run the risk that demotivated visitors will not be at the next sessions.

The conclusion which aims to address a call to action, can lead either to mental acceptance, or to hand gestures or standing up as a sign of total submission to God. The next chapter of this work "The Art of Obtaining Decisions", will deal in more detail with techniques related to the call.

2. Program Development

The program development should be done methodically, without breaks, without hesitation. The evangelistic campaign coordination should ensure that everything is well in place before the start of the program that those assigned to execute a point are present, and, if not, provide for their replacement.

No negligence should be tolerated at this stage: organists, ushers, songs, audio-visual supports, etc., everything should be in place before the start of the program to avoid the smallest false note. The preacher should also remember that, as the main character, all eyes are on him: his attire and his slightest gestures attract attention.

III- THE SERMON

The Sermon which could still be called "Homily", "Preach", and "Or exhortation", is the biblical message addressing an audience already initiated to Christian practices. This type of message generally aims at the consolidation of faith or any aspect of the believer's spiritual life.

We therefore understand that the sermon does not have the same objective as lay preaching. The development of different types of sermons is dealt with in the next section, presenting the classification of biblical messages about content.

III-a Topical or thematic sermon

The Topical or thematic sermon is one which, independently of the base texts, is oriented around a theme or subject; this theme thus becomes the basis of the Sermon; that is to say, the main sections or divisions of the Sermon will be inspired by this theme. This definition indicates that it is the subject or theme that is the basis of the sermon, and not a text or biblical passage. Although preaching practice leads the preacher to indicate a text at the beginning of his message, this is not at all obligatory and it is not this text that constitutes the substance of the sermon.

In this case, the different sections that constitute the framework of the sermon plan are supported by one or several biblical references, and any of these texts could be retained by the preacher as text annexed to the title, without being for all that the center of the sermon. In the topical sermon, the preacher, after defining the main theme, lists throughout the Bible the passages corresponding to this theme and thus establishes the outline or plan of the sermon. This approach refers to two (2) important points:

1. The obligation for the preacher to be a fervent and constant student of God's word, because it is in the field of these biblical consultations that he will find, in his subconscious, a set of passages, illustrations, and stories related to the theme he proposes to develop. That said, it is difficult for a preacher to experience this type of preaching if he was not first an assiduous reader of God's word.

2. The biblical passages are arranged to constitute the main sections or subdivisions of the message. However, this arrangement must be done according to a logical sequence to facilitate understanding by the listeners. This plan must take the form of a logical or chronological progression. For example, in dealing with the theme relating to sin, the preacher must present, in a logical sequence plan: the definition of sin, its first manifestation, its entry into the world, its consequences, and God's response to the problem of sin. The reverse presentation would be inappropriate; it would be like telling a story starting with the end.

Speaking of the topical sermon, Helge Stadelmann says:

"1- *The preacher must gather all the texts that relate to his theme in the Bible or the selected part of the Bible.*

2- The structure will emerge from the different aspects of biblical declarations about this theme

. 3- For each point, the preacher will gather a selection of biblical texts that will play the same role as the verses of the pericope of the expository sermon."

J. Dubois, in his homiletics course, seems to make a plea in favor of thematic preaching:

"*Today, the choice goes largely towards the theme. Our century likes to eat à la carte. We choose at the outset the menus that we think will best respond to our needs and our spiritual health. Thus, those who make the programs are concerned with offering a wide range of subjects and themes for reflection... Thematic preaching offers the advantage of making a complete tour of a question by taking examples and declarations from the whole biblical revelation... The thematic approach is indispensable whenever we want to study selectively or exhaustively a given subject in the Bible."*

It should be noted that thematic preaching is the ideal type of doctrinal sermon within the framework of lay preaching. When one wishes to address a theme related to a point of biblical doctrine, all the passages related to the said theme are identified throughout the Bible; then the structure of the message is built.

Example of a topical or thematic sermon

To illustrate this type of sermon, let us consider the case of a preacher who wants, in preaching, to exhort his audience about vigilance or preparation regarding the imminence of Jesus' return. The subject or theme retained is: "The proximity of Jesus' return: vigilance and preparation"

Thus, to prepare the outline or plan of his sermon, the preacher will list, throughout the Bible, all passages relating to his theme and constitute, thus, the following main sections or divisions of his sermon:

1. **The Bible's silence regarding the date of return: Mat 24:36**

2. **Precursor signs of return:** Mat 24:22,23

    a. **Political signs:** Mat 24:6-8

    b. **Moral signs:** 2Tim 3:1-5

    c. **Growing iniquity:** Mat 24:12

    d. **The mockers:** 2 Peter 3:3-4

3. **Call to vigilance:** Mat 24:42-44; 2 Peter 3:10-12

III-b Textual or expository sermon

The Textual or expository sermon is a sermon that draws inspiration from a biblical passage which can be part of a verse, an entire verse, or several verses. This definition allows us to note that it is the text or biblical passage that is the basis of the sermon and not the theme; this means that if the textual sermon has a theme, it is not the latter that will determine the orientation of the sermon. It is just the opposite; it is the passages targeted by the preaching that will lead to this theme. The preacher's first task consists of studying the whole biblical passage to find the main subject or theme.

It should be emphasized that there is no absolute or universal definition for the textual or expository sermon. The latter differs among authors dealing with homiletics. For James Braga, a sermon is textual only when it refers to a few verses (two or three), otherwise, one must speak of "sermon in the form of exposition" which he introduces in his classification of sermons. This opinion is not at all shared by certain authors, such as F.B. Meyer. For him, the valid criterion is not the length of the passage considered:

"Whatever the length of the section explained, if it is treated in such a way as to make clear its real and essential meaning, as it existed in the mind of the biblical author and light of the general context of Scripture and that this meaning is applied to the real needs of listeners, we can say that it is expository preaching."

L. M. Perry says that he has concluded: *"There are almost as many definitions of expository preaching as there are books written on this subject."* Sidney Greidanus goes further to speak of the confusion that reigns in the very diverse definitions of expository preaching. (See The Modern Preacher and the Ancient Text, pp 10-12, Grand Rapids Eerdmans, Leicester Inter-Varsity Press 1988).

On the other hand, two (2) advantages of the textual sermon enumerated by W. Evans should be highlighted:

"1- It produces preachers and listeners familiar with the Bible. It enriches both in the knowledge of the biblical text.

2- It conforms to the biblical model of preaching (cf. Jesus: Luke 4, Stephen: Acts 7, Paul: Acts 28, Peter: Acts 2 and 3"

Example of a textual or expository sermon Consider as base text: Philippians 1:27-29

v.27 "Only let your manner of life be worthy of the gospel of Christ, so that whether I come and see you or am absent, I may hear of you that you are standing firm in one spirit, with one mind striving side by side for the faith of the gospel (...)

v.28 (...) and not frightened in anything by your opponents. This is a clear sign to them of their destruction, but of your salvation (...)

v.29 (...) For it has been granted to you that for the sake of Christ, you should not only believe in him but also suffer for his sake."

It emerges that through this passage, Paul wants to exhort Christians in general, and the Philippians in particular, on four (4) essential points that can constitute the four guiding lines or sections of the sermon:

1. **Live worthily of the Gospel** (v. 27(a))
2. **Live the Gospel in unity** (v. 27(b))
3. **Live the Gospel during opposition** (v. 28)
4. **Suffer because of the Gospel** (v. 29)

The following remarks should be noted:

1. The preacher can, in analyzing the ideas expressed in these sections, place this sermon under the theme: "Being Christian, a way of life."

2. The preacher can reinforce or enrich the different sections with other texts or passages from the bible, not taken from the book of Philippians:

For example:

- **Section 1: Eph. 5:8,9** *"For at one time you were darkness, but now you are light in the Lord. Walk as children of light (for the fruit of light is found in all that is good and right and true)*

- **Section 2: Eph. 4:3,4** *"Eager to maintain the unity of the Spirit in the bond of peace. There is one body and one Spirit, just as you were called to the one hope that belongs to your call."*

- **Section 3: Heb.12:3** *"Consider him who endured from sinners such hostility against himself, so that you may not grow weary or fainthearted."*

- **Section 4: 1 Peter 1:6,7** *"In this you rejoice, though now for a little while, if necessary, you have been grieved by various trials... so that the tested genuineness of your faith—more precious than gold that perishes though it is tested by fire—may be found to result in praise and glory and honor at the revelation of Jesus Christ."*

III-c Narrative sermon

The Narrative sermon centers on the narration of a biblical fact that may involve events, persons, and actions. Narrative preaching has something in common with the textual and expository sermons; because they are both centered on biblical texts and passages, with the difference that the narrative sermon may concern a longer passage of Scripture one or several chapters of Holy Scripture.

This form of preaching, according to George Bass, is more recent than the others and began to take shape in the early 1970s. Treating biblical narratives, narrative preaching can refer to several types in the Bible, such as parables, prophecies, etc. We remember, for example, Jesus' meeting with the Samaritan woman (John 4:1-42); the sickness, death, and resurrection of Lazarus (John 11:1-46); the story of the three young Hebrews in the court of Babylon (Daniel 3:1-30), etc.

Alfred Kuen indicates the forms that a narrative sermon can take:

"Narrative preaching can also take various forms: a biblical or contemporary narrative (or both), with or without a theme, developed in a deductive or inductive manner, following the chronological development of the story or beginning in the middle or at the end of the story and then returning to the beginning... One can also start by telling a biblical story in its setting, then take it up again in a contemporary form to show its current application. One can begin by posing the problem using a current story followed by a biblical story that gives the solution to the problem."

The story's narration must lead the preacher to discover or detect spiritual applications to achieve this objective. In a word, lessons must be drawn from the story being told. For S. Greidanus:

"The narrator seeks to proclaim God's word from the past in the present situation; this word inscribed in the Bible has a normative point (a theme) that must be transferred to the present. It is not enough to tell a story and leave its interpretation to the listeners. A sermon is something other than an aesthetic experience; as God's message, it must leave no doubt as to its specific meaning. David would have completely missed the point of Nathan's story if he had not added: "You are that man (2 Sam 12:7)".

However, the same biblical narrative can lead different preachers to discover different spiritual lessons and applications, depending on their inspirations. For example, the narrative of 1 Kings 18 and 19, relating the experience of the prophet Elijah on Mount Carmel and involving Ahab, Jezebel, the prophet, and the prophets of Baal, is an illustration that can be the subject of a narrative sermon. A preacher can draw several aspects from this narrative to prepare a truly edifying sermon.

In summary, among the three (3) types of sermons exposed in this chapter: Topical Sermon, Textual Sermon, and Narrative Sermon, one cannot affirm that there is one that is superior to the other. All three pursue the same objective "change in the heart". The preacher will apply, according to circumstances and his abilities, such a given type of preaching.

This brings us to the end of Chapter 6, which has covered the main classifications and types of biblical messages. Each type serves its purpose and can be effective when properly used according to the circumstances, the audience, and the message to be conveyed.

Each type has its strengths:

- Topical sermons are excellent for addressing specific themes comprehensively

- Textual sermons help maintain a close connection with Scripture

- Narrative sermons can make biblical truths more engaging and memorable

The key is for the preacher to understand these different types well enough to choose the most appropriate one for each specific preaching occasion, while always keeping the central goal in mind: transformation of hearts through the power of God's Word.

CHAPTER 7 - THE SECTIONS OF A SERMON PLAN

The objective aimed at by every preacher should be clarity, logic, and coherence in the presentation or exposition of his message. But this approach begins already from the conception of the plan which is the main guide of the exposition. For this, the message should never be conceived as a block, but rather divided into sections or divisions. Each section of the plan is thus a way of grouping ideas relating to specific portions of the message. This way of proceeding is a guide not only for the preacher, but also for the audience who can better understand the contours of a message divided into sections, and where ideas are expressed distinctly.

7.1- Importance of Sections for The Preacher

The examples presented above, in the outline of topical and textual sermons, already suggest the idea of dividing the sermon into different sections. Each section develops a specific aspect of the sermon, and this aspect is supported and backed by one or a group of verses.

Thus, there is no way for the preacher to get confused, during his exposition, in considerations that are sometimes inappropriate. The different portions of the sermon, planned in the outline, must be presented, and logically, and in a way that contributes to the overall understanding of the theme considered. The conception of a sermon plan in sections is first a sure guide for the preacher himself who can easily move from one point to another of his plan, without breaks, without interruption, and without this transition being noticed by the assembly.

Another point to consider is that the ideas expressed in a sermon plan must be presented in a logical order to facilitate understanding and assimilation. For example, in the model of the topical sermon, presented in a previous chapter (Proximity of Jesus' return: vigilance and preparation), how would you judge the sermon plan where the preacher would present the outline of different sections thus:

1. Call to vigilance and preparation
2. The signs of Jesus' return
3. The Bible's silence and the date of return

This would be like someone wanting to build a house starting from the top and not from the base. A logical presentation would be:

a. The reality of the return (date known or not)

b. The signs indicating this proximity

c. The necessity of spiritual preparation and a call to vigilance

It should also be emphasized that the preacher whose message plan is not conceived in sections or divisions is already preparing a weak and ineffective presentation. During this presentation, ideas are expressed in an unordered way and without coherence. This often leads to cases where the preacher has great difficulty concluding his message and, consequently, ends up with a presentation of too long duration that tires and demotivates the assembly.

7.2 Importance of Sections for The Assembly

The main victim of the presentation of a sermon not organized in sections is the assembly. Often, after having participated in a worship service, one asks someone from the assembly their impressions of the sermon. They might respond, sometimes: "the preacher preached well; he delivered a very beautiful message" but, when asked to recall the main points of this message, they say they cannot do so, because they vaguely remember what was said. One can thus understand what happened: the preacher spoke about everything at once without highlighting the key ideas of his sermon. In a word, he did not divide his message into sections. In short, the assembly did not retain the essential part of an exhortation that could have been a great blessing for them.

CHAPTER 8 - CONCEPTION OF THE SERMON

Nicolas Boileau already said quite well: *"What is well conceived can be clearly stated and the words to say it come easily."* The conception of the message automatically refers to the preparation of the message and leads to the question: "Should one prepare one's message?" The imperative answer is: yes!

Presenting oneself before an audience to speak in the name of the Creator is one of the greatest and highest responsibilities that can be entrusted to a human. It is an honor and a formidable task. The preacher who does it should respect himself and respect his audience, and respect for this audience must pass through the concern to present something of good quality. Not to do so is to treat this audience with contempt and dishonor God. In a word, one must prepare one's message. The preacher may find himself, on an exceptional occasion, having to preach a message without preparation: this is the case of an improvisation where one must replace someone who was programmed and absent. The exception does not destroy, nor replace the rule.

The following **eight (8) points** should guide the preacher in the preparation of his message:

1. Source of Inspiration of the Sermon:

A preacher can find, anywhere, the source of inspiration for his sermon. It might be a biblical verse spotted during a reading, part of a verse, an article from a religious newspaper, the text of a song, etc. The text and melody of a song that was transmitted to me by a friend on WhatsApp inspired me to deliver a powerful message about an episode in Jesus' life. A message can be inspired by a sermon preached by another preacher on radio, television, or at a weekly worship service. A homiletics specialist went further to declare that we can not only be inspired by the messages of others but preach the preaching of others. Rudolf Bohren in his work: "Preaching Another's Preaching" writes:

"Not every theologian has the gift of preaching. A less gifted preacher will have better influence if he considers good preaching from a peer than if he fails with poor preaching of his own... With time perhaps will grow the ease, the courage of a personal speech, the sovereign freedom to modify and structure"

Further on, J. Adams declares: *"We all borrow... The only question is: How to imitate, who and what to imitate?"*. What is important is to use these borrowings as materials that one uses to build a product that is truly our own. Imitating or preaching another's preaching must never be a replica or reproduction of the message written by the other preacher, neither in substance nor in form.

2. Prayer

Prayer is an important point in message preparation, the preacher should strive to seek divine inspiration in a) The choice of theme to develop and which can have the most impact on hearts. b) The identification and research of biblical passages that illuminate said theme.

The fact of touching hearts is the work of the Holy Spirit. The preacher should, in all humility, remember that he is the channel through which God speaks to others. Consequently, he must seek God's help, through prayer, not only for the conception of the message but also for the way to expose it: the right tone, the attitude, and the appropriate gestures. In a word, the preacher believes in the power of prayer.

3. Bible Reading

Assiduous: Reading the Bible is a field that provides the preacher with the necessary materials for preparing his messages. If for the ordinary Christian, reading the bible each year (the Old and New Testament) is a good thing, this is even more so for the preacher, one who, either periodically or about his function, is called to occupy the pulpit quite often to proclaim God's Word. But, for him, it must never be a mechanical and hasty reading; as if to have the conscience of having read, during the year, almost the whole Bible. This means that the reading suggested here is active. This means that, while reading, one must often stop on passages, verses, and illustrations; ruminate on them, and penetrate them. One must often make annotations, and take notes. Many ideas or message themes can arise from this kind of reading.

Besides reading the Bible, the preacher must lead a life of study, and be an eternal student. Cultivating oneself in the greatest possible number of domains is an obligation for a preacher who wants to stay up to date on the major questions that arise at the world level.

4. Duration of Sermon:

Preparation This leads to asking the question: How long does it take to prepare a message? While recognizing that there is no absolute answer to this question, one can generally affirm that preparation must not be rushed. "Usually, says Spurgeon, coming to the pulpit without having prepared is an unforgivable presumption"

J. Stott declares *"A beginner will need ten (10) to twelve (12) hours to prepare a message."* D. Bonhoeffer indicates that: *"Twelve hours of work on a sermon is a good rule"* and J. Stott adds that it takes at least *"One hour of preparation for every five minutes of the sermon"*

5. Choice of a Text, Is It Mandatory?

If practice has suggested reading a base text at the beginning of a sermon, it should be emphasized that a beginning text is not always necessary if one wants to preach a topical or thematic message. In the latter case, it is the retained theme that determines the choice of verses that will be considered to support the different sections of the message. The other trap to avoid is to choose a base text (in the case of a textual sermon) and talk about all other things, without sufficiently exploiting the specific text considered.

But, if one must choose a base text, which one to choose? We have already emphasized that assiduous reading of the Bible offers the preacher an abundance of texts that cross his mind and that could eventually suit the theme he proposes to develop. At this stage, one must sort, and choose among several.

6. The Sermon Plan:

A written plan is needed. Ideas must be expressed according to a certain order and one must respect this plan and master it well. Your plan must be complete including an introduction, development, and conclusion.

7. Sermon Theme:

The theme or title of the message should have two (2) main characteristics:

a- Appropriate to the message: It happens sometimes that a preacher develops a message that has very little or no relation to the retained theme. In this case, even after the exposition, the audience remains unsatisfied, insofar as it is the title of the message that arouses their interest. In a word, the title of the message must have a well-determined relationship with the message.

c. Concise: Concision should guide the preacher in the choice of theme. If it is true that a theme consisting of a long phrase is inappropriate, it is also true that a theme consisting of a single word can lack clarity. One must not sacrifice clarity for concision.

8. The Introduction:

Through the introduction, the preacher intends to prepare the minds of his listeners and ensure that the message he wants to communicate will be captured and understood. The introduction aims to awaken the assembly's interest in the chosen subject. In general, one introduces the subject with general order declarations that make an impression on people to awaken this interest. The preacher should pay much attention to the very important and very first minutes of the sermon. By his way of doing this, he can gain or lose the attention of his audience; and lose the good disposition that they could have brought to the sermon. However, a fundamental difference between introduction and preliminaries must be emphasized.

Preliminaries consist of all declarations, information, and greetings, made at the beginning of the message and which have no relation to the theme that will be developed. Care will certainly be taken that these are not too long and thus infringe on the time reserved for the introduction and development.

CHAPTER 9 - EXPOSITION OF THE SERMON

A well-conceived sermon does not necessarily ensure an effective oral presentation; this is where the preacher's qualities related to communication or his art of preaching must come into play. Here, we will retain nine (9) elements that should guide this presentation.

1. Preaching Without Written Guide:

This comes down to asking the question: "Should one preach without notes or plan?" Remember that the exposition of the message, to be effective and produce the desired effects, requires a logical, orderly, and structured presentation. But this structuring cannot be the work of memory or chance. A written plan is needed where the main ideas are expressed. It is this plan that will indicate the different sections of the message.

Moreover, to justify the existence of a written guide (notes and plan), it must be remembered that the same message can be preached several times. Preaching without a written guide is to lose the memory of this message. However, it should be noted in passing that the effective preacher will never be a slave to his notes or written supports; he will maintain constant visual contact with his audience.

2. Can one read One's Sermon?

Regarding the reading of a sermon, two (2) cases must be highlighted:

- A sermon written by the preacher himself

- A sermon written by another preacher

- **Sermon written by the preacher himself**

Some preachers choose not only to have a detailed sermon plan but also an exhaustive and very advanced development of the different parts of this sermon, to the point of taking on the appearance of a speech. This approach is not at all recommended, as it prevents visual contact with the audience, which is so indispensable for effective communication of God's Word. Such a preacher is necessarily a slave to his text. If one must write one's sermon, one must nevertheless submit to certain rules or principles:

1. Do not develop in detail all parts of the sermon; that is to say, leave room for personal punctual interventions, which facilitates connection with the assembly during the exposition.

2. Write the sermon in an oral style and not in a written style. There is a fundamental difference between the two styles: the written style is much more concise, and colder, with fewer or no repetitions; while in the oral style, one can always refer to what was already said and make repetitions often so indispensable to orality and sermon communication. One can even intersperse interactions with listeners and even calls. In summary, writing in an oral style is to represent oneself speaking while writing the text.

On this subject, here is what Alfred Kuen recommends:

"Write large enough that one can read at a distance of about 50 cm. The structure of the message must appear clearly. Make small paragraphs easy to supervise. Underline the first words of each in color (to avoid returning twice in a row to the same sub-point). Put keywords in large writing."

- **Sermon written by another preacher:**

In certain circumstances, a preacher may have to preach a sermon written by someone else. This is the case, for example, of messages prepared for special prayer weeks: Week on Unity and Family Consolidation, Youth Activities Promotion Week, Annual Prayer Week, etc. On these occasions, messages prepared in advance by special preachers are transmitted to local fields to be preached by speakers chosen for the circumstance. Such a message should never be "read" before an assembly, but "preached"; that is to say, not take over exactly the content of the written message.

Some preachers make the mistake of reading such a text before an audience, from beginning to end and often repeating the same terms as the initial preacher. One ends up with a bland, boring and lifeless presentation. In this case, one has not preached; rather one has just done a good reading exercise. Here is the advice to apply for the exposition of a sermon written by another preacher:

1. Reread the message text several times underlining or selecting, in strong ink, the different parts on which you want to focus your sermon. It is not necessary to repeat all the details, verses and all the parts treated by the one who wrote the initial text.

2. Deepen the retained and underlined parts, referring, if needed, to other biblical passages or other illustrations, not indicated in the initial document.

3. Consolidate everything in a new plan that will be developed and exposed before the assembly.

Thus, this message presented to the assembly will be "your sermon", passed through your mold, and not that of the preacher who prepared the initial message. In exposing such a message, you will have more self-confidence and be able to easily detach yourself from your manuscript, and make a positive impact on your audience. In summary, a sermon written by another preacher must be "a pretext" or a basis for preaching your sermon.

To formally answer the question: *"Can one read one's sermon?"*, *we will say, here, that, if it is true that God can use a written and read sermon to touch hearts, there is, however, nothing more painful than a speaker who reads his entire sermon; whether it is a sermon written by him personally or by another preacher.*

Such a position is supported by Francis Vanoye who, in his work "Expression Communication" affirms that an exposition read instead of being said: *"cannot be followed by the audience"*:

- Because the information brought by a written text is far too numerous, while the information brought by a spoken text is diluted in redundancies, repetitions, pauses and, thereby, much more accessible;

- Because reading "erases" the personality of the speaker, who no longer looks at his audience and cuts himself off from the group;

- Because reading excludes the indispensable non-verbal modes of communication for maintaining contact: looks, gestures, bodily expression"

3. The Duration of the Sermon

The question to ask here is the following: "Is there an ideal duration for a sermon?"

From the outset, it must be answered that there is no optimal duration applicable to all sermons and in all circumstances. In general, the duration of a sermon may depend on three (3) factors:

a. The circumstance:

A homily at a marriage ceremony or an exhortation at a funeral service will not be of the same duration as a sermon at a weekly worship service. In the first case, it is about addressing some advice to the spouses and some words of comfort to bereaved families. An intervention of fifteen to twenty minutes must amply suffice. The same applies to a mid-week meeting where the congregation gathers to pray and spiritually refresh themselves. This is a rather brief message. On the other hand, at worship service, the audience expects a longer, more substantial message, with concrete applications to daily life.

b. The dispositions of the congregation:

This refers to the listening habits of the congregation. A preacher, before taking the pulpit before an assembly, should first inquire about the practice of sermon duration generally expected in this community. In some environments, a sermon of 30 to 45 minutes is acceptable and desirable; on the other hand, a message approaching 60 minutes would indispose this same audience. Yet, certain religious communities are accustomed to sermons of at least an hour.

One must also consider the age of most people present. Elderly or sick people do not have the same capacity for concentration as young people. In a word, the preacher must be a psychologist.

c. The interest aroused by the sermon:

The preacher in the pulpit should be able to evaluate, at any moment, the degree of receptivity or attention to his message. Not all sermons arouse the same interest. In this regard, here is what Wolfgang Klippert declares:

"With certain preachers, everyone consults their watch after a quarter of an hour; with others, one is quite surprised that forty minutes have passed when they announce their conclusion. This is why each preacher should get used to observing the reactions of his listeners and evaluating the time during which they listen to him attentively." (A. Kuen, C.P., p. 184)

"The best way to shorten a sermon, said H. W. Beecher, is to make it more interesting"

4. Humor in Preaching:

Can one use humor in preaching? In a word, can the preacher cause or incite his audience to laugh during his exposition? Nothing seems to prevent such a practice, and this is in no way contrary to the propriety that should characterize the solemnity of worship. However, humor must be used wisely:

1. It must reflect a natural impulse in the preacher who is not trying to imitate others. Some people are naturally inclined to make people laugh and it suits them well, some other people are incapable of it and would appear ridiculous in attempting to do so.

2. The preacher should avoid creating or forging stories with the sole purpose of amusing or relaxing his assembly. In this case, he displays poor taste: he lies, which is contrary not only to the dignity of the pulpit but also and especially to the moral and spiritual values that must characterize a preacher.

Humor can have certain advantages, in the sense that it breaks tension. Many listeners can hardly maintain mental concentration or emotional pressure during a sermon. They need to relax for a moment.

5. The Tract and Preaching:

Speaking in front of a group of people for the first time, or even often, is always a stressful situation. Astute observers recognize that people who, during their childhood or adolescence, are used to speaking in public, express themselves more easily in these circumstances. Religious communities generally offer such an opportunity to children and young people.

But whatever the context considered; stage fright is a normal phenomenon among all those who are called to speak in public. Cicero declared:

"The most skillful orator, the one who expresses himself with the most elegance and facility, is in my eyes only brazen if he does not tremble when mounting the tribune, and if he does not tremble again during his entire exordium". (De Oratore I 26)

This is also true for someone who must stand behind a pulpit to speak in the name of God. A. Kuen says:

"Stage fright in itself is not a bad sign, especially in someone who must announce God's oracles. It is such a formidable task that it is normal that a sacred fear, sometimes even: a sacred fright seizes you now of mounting the pulpit".

Experienced speakers give certain advice to overcome this stress:

- Breathe deeply
- Look calmly at the assembly

6. Appropriate bodily expression

If we speak with the mouth, we do so well also with the body; and body language greatly reinforces that of speech.

"In ordinary conversation with a friend, we accompany our words with appropriate gestures. Body language is part of the symbolic conventions

that everyone understands, even without words. Why wouldn't we use the same natural gestures in the pulpit?... Everything that brings a message closer to a familiar conversation favors communication. Our gestures underline what we want to say, they awaken the attention of listeners and facilitate their concentration."

But if gestures are important, one must however well avoid excessive and inappropriate gestures that an author calls parasitic gestures. In this sense, Jean Bosch says this:

"If impassive immobility is detestable, nervous agitation is even more so...The pulpit is neither a carpenter's workbench nor a fairground, let us therefore avoid swaying back and forth or even from left to right."

If bodily expression suits the exposition of the message well, one must however avoid falling into the other extreme: making theater.

"Do not encourage men who must engage in this work to imagine that they must theatrically proclaim the sacred message. Nothing should be introduced into our work that has the appearance of a spectacle. God's cause must have a sacred, heavenly imprint... Some, believing they could accomplish effective work, have adopted curious behavior, and indulged in eccentricities. Do not approve of this kind of thing. These exploits which had a theatrical appearance are not in their place when we proclaim the solemn messages that have been entrusted to us."

7. Visual Contact with The Audience

To establish this visual contact with the audience, one must try to detach, as much as possible from one's manuscript; and no longer be its slave. Visual contact with the assembly is important in more than one way. Wolfgang Klippert indicates to us at least two (2) advantages:

1. It creates an atmosphere of openness and personal proximity. It facilitates the encounter between the person of the preacher and that of the listeners. A speaker who does not look at those who listen to him appears distant and reserved; his message is too.

2. Visual contact gives the preacher the possibility to react to signals emanating from his audience. A sermon is a constant

dialogue: on one side, words and gestures, on the other, body language."

Concerning this visual contact with the audience, Jean Bosch says:

"Nothing is more embarrassing than a preacher for whom only his notes seem to exist, a nail in the wall, the shoes of people in the first row, or the hats in the galleries"

8. ChristoCentrism:

The preacher must preach Jesus Christ. Whatever the nature of the message, one should always strive to draw attention to the one who is the way, the truth, and the life. All true doctrine places Christ at the center of its teaching. A Bible study, a lay preaching, or a sermon should never take place without drawing the listeners' attention to the Lamb of God who takes away the sins of the world.

9. General Advice Relating to Message Exposition

During the exposition or presentation of the message, the preacher should:

1. Maintain interest, and capture the attention of the audience from beginning to end.
2. Avoid breaks in expression (no interruptions).
3. Speak with vigor, vitality, and conviction.
4. Avoid speaking unnaturally.
5. Have good pronunciation.
6. Watch the flow of the message.

The flow should be neither too slow nor too rapid. Practice alone, by recording and listening to yourself. This method has the advantage of making you control the duration of the message.

CHAPTER 10 - SEQUENCE OF SUBJECTS

The point treated here refers exclusively to the planning of a series of Bible studies and a series of public evangelical conferences or lay preaching. Whatever the number of themes or subjects retained, the strong point of planning lies in the order of subjects, the sequence according to which they will be presented or exposed.

This series should always begin with subjects or themes of general order, those that interest everyone and which are not controversial, for example: God's love, repentance, the Word of God, etc. Gradually, one can move on to more complex subjects, difficult to accept. It would be a misstep on the part of a preacher to begin a series with a subject that generally raises contradictions and opposition.

The Gospel must be presented like a great chain where each subject represents a link that is connected to another. The people who participate in this series must discover the logic and beauty of this chain. It is even good practice that at the end of each exposition, the title of the next subject is announced, a way to arouse visitors' curiosity.

Making a mistake in the sequence of subjects is to break the chain and break its strength. That said, the truth of the Gospel must be presented link after link, line after line so that it appears as a logical chain whose links are connected.

However, it should be emphasized that this requirement in the sequence or order of subjects is not as rigorous when it comes to a series of sermons to be presented to an assembly of believers, people already initiated to the Gospel. This is the case for example of a series to be preached during a certain number of days (7, 21, 30, 40 days) and whose themes aim first at: strengthening, consolidation, and revival. In these cases, whatever sequence is considered, the effect produced on hearts by each presentation will always be the same.

CHAPTER 11 - THE BIBLE SPEAKS: SERIES OF BIBLE STUDIES

We have inserted in this work this evangelical tool: a Series of Bible studies, which intends to be a base for teaching and learning. That said, it can serve either the preacher or the Bible student himself who can, alone, deepen basic biblical doctrines. The presentation of each study greatly favors this objective, because:

1. It gives, at the beginning of each one, a brief introduction that orients the theme considered.

2. For each question considered, the essential aspects of the cited verses are developed and notes or comments are recorded.

The reference verses cited in this series are taken from the Louis Segond version.

STUDY #1: WHAT IS THE BIBLE?

What book is the Bible? The most popular book, the most read throughout the world, and the most attacked through the ages, and which has resisted the test of time. According to a publication of "Wycliffe Global Alliance" in October 2019, the Bible is translated into more than 3384 languages.

The word "Bible" which is not found in the Bible comes from the Greek "biblia" translated as "books". In a word, the Bible is a collection of books grouped in two (2) parts called Testaments (the Old and New Testament); it is called indifferently, the Word of God, Holy Scripture, Holy Scriptures, Holy letters (2 Timothy 3:15). The Bible is at the center of all religious groups that claim Christianity. The first question that one asks about a book and which gives it all its authority and credit, is the following: Who is its author?

Where does the Bible come from? Who is its author? How did it reach humanity and why? So many questions that, imperatively, must have an answer insofar as all subjects of this series will be based on this book.

1. **What is said about the Word of God? John 17:17; Psalms 119:160**

   "Sanctify them by your truth: Your Word is truth" John 17:17

   "The foundation of your word is truth." Psalms 119:160(a)

   - *Here is a powerful word "truth" to which all those who want to approach God in all sincerity attach themselves. God's word is truth. To find this truth, one must read, study, and search the Bible. This truth is found neither in religious Confessions nor in human philosophies.*

2. **Who inspired the Holy Scriptures? 2 Timothy 3:16**

   "All Scripture is inspired by God" v.16(a)

   - *The inspiration of the Bible is divine; the author of the Bible is God. To accept the prescripts of the Bible is to accept God and not the biblical writer whose passage bears the name (Matthew, James, Isaiah, etc.). To reject the Bible is to reject or dishonor God, and not the one who is its spokesperson.*

3. **Who wrote the pages of the Bible? 2 Peter 1:20,21**

   "But men spoke from God as they were carried along by the Holy Spirit." 2 Peter 1:21(a)

   - *To make God's Word (the Bible) accessible to humanity, God used human means: prophets; but men influenced or moved by the Holy Spirit. That said, it was not their word, but God's word transmitted by them, through their intermediary.*
   - *The Bible which is a compilation of 66 books (39 in the Old Testament and 27 in the New), was written by 40 biblical writers,*

from Moses who wrote the Pentateuch to the Apostle John who wrote Revelation.

- *The Bible was written by prophets who did not all live in the same era and who are of different education and social levels; yet, their writings do not contradict each other and form such a harmonious whole that even the most skeptical are forced to recognize that they were all inspired by the same Spirit, the Holy Spirit.*

- *The original text of the Bible was written in three languages:*

- *"There are no different types of Bibles: The Bible is unique; there are certainly several versions or translations of the original text. However, it should be emphasized that at the Council of Trent in 1546, the Catholic Church decided to introduce seven books in the Old Testament namely: Tobit, Wisdom, Sirach, Baruch, 1 and 2 Maccabees and some chapters added to the books of Esther and Daniel. These are historical books whose authors are Hebrew, but they are not recognized as part of the Sacred Canon. The Catholic Church has called them 'Deuterocanonical books', of second inspiration"; non-Catholic Christians qualify them as 'apocryphal books', that is to say inauthentic."* **Juan A. Bonjour, The Bible Answers, p.15, Edition 1991**

- *The Biblical Canon: The word "Canon" from the Greek Kanôn is drawn from the Hebrew "qaneh" which means "reed, measure, cane". In Antiquity, it was a measuring instrument made with a reed, like a carpenter's or mason's rule (Ez. 40:3; Rev. 21:15). In the figurative sense, it means the rule of conduct, the norm, the model. Applied to God's word, the word canon designates the norm to which the teaching and life of God's people must conform. In the Bible, the canonical books are examined and measured before being accepted as the inspired word of God (see Dt. 18:15-22; 13:1-5; Is. 8:20).*

The canonical biblical books are the rule of doctrine for all believers. They have authority over their conduct. The canonical books have no contradictory teachings. There is doctrinal harmony between their writings even if the authors lived in different epochs.

The 39 books of the Hebrew Bible are declared canonical at the end of the first century AD. In 90 AD, Jewish rabbis formed an academy to determine the books that received the seal of divine inspiration. Christians of the New Covenant followed the same path to admit into the canon the 27 books of the New Testament. It was around 200 AD that the idea of fixing the New Testament canon emerged. At the end of this process, a canon of 27 books was formed.

The Apocryphal books: The word "apocryphal" means "hidden, added". These writings are called apocryphal because they are suspect both in their origin and their claimed doctrinal value. Under the instigation of Pope Paul III, the Roman Catholic Church canonized seven books: Tobit, Judith, 1 and 2 Maccabees, Baruch, Wisdom, Ecclesiasticus and two additions: addition to the book of Esther (chapter 8, Jerusalem Bible) and additions to the book of Daniel (chapters 13 and 14, Jerusalem Bible).

Why are the apocryphal books not admitted into the Old Testament Canon? And, why are they not part of Protestant versions? The teachings of the apocryphal books are in contradiction with the 39 canonical books of the Old Testament and the 27 canonical books of the New Testament. The apocryphal writings were not admitted into the Jewish canon because they do not have in them the proof of divine inspiration. They can be read and studied as a literary work that allows understanding of the four centuries when there were no prophets among the Jewish people. Here are some examples:

1. ***Tobit 4:10*** *"For alms deliver from death, and it prevents going into darkness"*

2. ***Tobit 12:9*** *"For alms save from death and purge away all sin. Those who give alms are satisfied with days;"*

- These writings which teach salvation by works are in contradiction with the Bible which teaches that the human being is saved by grace.

3. ***2 Maccabees 12:44-45*** *"For if he had not hoped that those who had fallen should rise again, it would have been superfluous and vain to pray for the dead, and if he envisaged that a very beautiful reward is reserved for those who fall asleep in piety, this was a holy and pious thought. This is why he had*

this expiatory sacrifice made for the dead, so that they might be delivered from their sin."

- *This book of Maccabees indicates that one can pray for the dead in contradiction with all biblical teaching (Ecclesiastes 9:5)*

    4. ***Ecclesiasticus 3:3*** *"He who honors his father expiates his sins."*

- *As general information about the Bible, it should be remembered:*
- *a. the shortest verse: John 11:35*
- *b. the longest verse: Esther 8:9*
- *c. the longest chapter: Psalm 119*
- *d. the shortest chapter: Psalm 117*

4. Why is it important to study the Word of God?

a. It enlightens: Psalms 119:105

"Your word is a lamp to my feet and a light to my path."

- *Lamp and light: two (2) symbols that well define what God's word does. It enlightens, it shows the way, it guides whoever wants to obey God. Any religious practice or doctrine that does not have a scriptural basis must be rejected.*

b. It reveals the future: Isaiah 46:9,10

"I announce from the beginning what will happen and long in advance what is not yet accomplished; I say: My decrees will stand, and I will execute all my will" v.10

- *God alone can predict and unveil the future. The Bible predicted the emergence and fall of universal world empires: Babylon, Medes and Persia, Greece, and Rome. All this was realized with rare accuracy (see Daniel 7:1-28). God alone also knows our future individually. The theory that by studying zodiac signs (astrology), someone can reveal our future is a pretentious aberration and a real deception. This practice is widely spread, nowadays, among those who attach themselves to horoscopes.*

c. It is spiritual food: Matthew 4:4; Deut. 8:1-3

"Jesus answered: It is written: Man shall not live by bread alone, but by every word that proceeds from the mouth of God" Matt 4:4

- Just as our body needs to be nourished by "physical" bread to keep us alive and healthy, our soul also needs to be nourished spiritually to stay alive. Thus, the Bible must not be a book to consult by chance or occasionally, but a source where one regularly draws to find God's directives and receive strength, support and consolation.

d. It preserves us from sin: Psalms 119:9,11

"I store your word in my heart, so that I might not sin against you." v.11

- To sin is to disobey God or infringe His will. The Bible, by revealing this will to us, becomes a mirror where we see ourselves as we are. The Psalmist says he stores this word in his heart not to sin against God; this is what we all are called to do.

5. **What can God's Word provide to the believer? (Eternal life: John 5:39)**

"You search the Scriptures because you think you have eternal life in them: they are they which testify of me"

- *Man was created to lead a life of eternal happiness. Sin hindered God's plan for humanity. The Bible teaches us that by approaching God through obedience, and accepting God's plan for our redemption this eternal life can be found again.*

6. **What should be our attitude toward God's Word? (Study it carefully: Acts 17:11,12)** "And they examined the Scriptures daily to see if what they were told was exact"

- *It is not enough to read the Bible as one does for an ordinary book; it is not enough to piously hear the proclamation of this word; one must search it, deepen it, and examine it, as did the Jews of Berea.*

7. What famine has been predicted? Amos 8:11,12

"Behold, the days are coming, says the Lord God, when I will send a famine on the land, not a famine of bread, nor a thirst for water, but of hearing the words of the Lord" v.11

- This word often despised and rejected nowadays, will be sought at some point, like gold; but the Bible declares: "They shall wander to and from to seek the word of the Lord, and shall not find it," v.12

8. What is said concerning certain things revealed in God's word? What do the ignorant sometimes do, and with what results? 2 Peter 3:16-18

"As he does in all his letters when he speaks of these things, in which are some things hard to understand, which untaught and unstable people twist to their destruction, as they do also the rest of the Scriptures" v.16

- The study of God's Word must be approached with prayer and humility. The Bible explains itself. A Bible text, to be understood, must be considered in its context and connected to other passages of the Bible. It is often said: "A text without context is a pretext"

9. What is said of the duration of God's Word? Isaiah 40:8 "

The grass withers, the flower fades, but the word of our God stands forever"

- God's word does not change with time and circumstances, but it is man who must adapt to it. It remains forever. Attacked through the ages, it still stands.

10. Is the Bible in contradiction with science?

- *The Bible is not a book of science, because science evolves, searches, and improves while the Bible is a completed book that resists the test of time. Yet the Bible is not foreign to science; it is the source of true science. Men believed for a long time that the earth was flat until more thorough observations demonstrated that it is rather round. When men of science recognize it, it is to give reason to the Bible which, long before, had spoken of the "circle of the earth". "It is He who sits above the circle of the earth" Isaiah 40:22*

- *The Bible indicated long ago that air is heavy has weight, before men of science had discovered that a liter of air ways' 1.2 gr. (wind is air in motion). "When He gave to the wind its weight and fixed the measure of the waters" Job 28:25. In a word, true science is not in contradiction with the Bible.*

RECAP: THEMES FOR REFLECTION DRAWN FROM THIS STUDY

1. Inspiration of God's Word

2. Writing of the Bible and original languages

3. Importance of Bible study

4. Duration of God's Word

5. The Bible and science

STUDY #2: CREATION AND EVOLUTION

Before talking about creation, the main theme of today's study, let us first recall the content of another concept: "Evolution or Evolutionism". The Big Bang: an explosion bursts by chance in the cosmos and all the planets appear and life begins to manifest fortuitously, without any external influence. This life, initially rudimentary, evolves over millions of years, before reaching its perfected level: man. This theory is, in general, the preserve of atheistic materialists. Charles Darwin, an Englishman, in his famous book "The Origin of Species" published in 1859, developed, and supported the theory of Evolution.

Any astute observer can note at least three (3) contradictions or inconsistencies in the theory of Evolution, according to which everything evolved.

1. These men, called scientists, say they do not believe in miracles, in chance. Everything can be explained by a

relationship of cause and effect, by mathematical formulas; yet the big bang would be the greatest miracle that has ever taken place. One must have a lot of faith to believe in it (First inconsistency).

2. Science, in whose name these men speak, establishes the notion of biogenesis, that is, life can only come from life. A living cell must decompose to give birth to other living cells. That said, the theory of spontaneous generation of Evolution is in flagrant contradiction with science. Therefore, this theory is not scientific (Second inconsistency).

3. If human beings evolved over millions of years before reaching the current stage of man, why is this evolution blocked upon reaching the current stage of man? (Third inconsistency).

On the other hand, being believers, we have made the Bible the basis of our faith; Let us see, within the framework of this study, what it says about creation.

1. **Who created the heavens and the earth, and when? Genesis 1:1, 2**

"In the beginning, God created the heavens and the earth" v.1

- *"In the beginning God created": This expression is a challenge launched to man of all times. To create is to bring forth from nothing, to bring into existence from nothing. Man has never created. He has only invented and studied what exists from God's creation to formulate laws.*

- *"The Bible's creation account is a challenge to the theory of evolution according to which man descends from the ape and that life appeared on earth millions of years ago through the play of physicochemical forces operating according to the laws of chance. According to this theory, life materialized, first, under rudimentary appearances, then gradually became more complex over the ages, still according to the laws of chance. Living forms transformed themselves (...) species gave birth to other species different from the first, better organized." (Jean Flori and Henri RasolofoMasoandro,*

Creation and Evolution, p. 15; SDT Edition, Dammarie-les-Lys, France, 1974)

2. **What did God do on the first day of creation? Genesis 1:3-5 (Light)**

"Let there be light! and there was light" v.3 "God called the light Day, and the darkness he called Night. And there was evening and there was morning: the first day" v.5

- *It should be noted here, through these passages that: 1- Light existed even before the creation of the sun which will be done on the fourth day of creation. 2- Each day of creation consisted of an evening and a morning literal day of twenty-four (24) hours and not symbolic days of a thousand (1,000) years, as claimed by certain theories circulated nowadays by certain contradictors of God's Word.*

3. **What did God do on the second day of creation? Genesis 1:6-8, Heaven (expanse)**

"And God said, let there be an expanse between the waters to separate water from water... God called the expanse Heaven."

- **Heaven,** here, is defined as the visible expanse above the ground from the earth's surface, from horizon to zenith, in which meteors are observed (thunder, lightning, rain, snow, and hail) and the regular movements of celestial bodies (moon, sun, stars, etc.). Heaven is both the earth's atmosphere in which birds fly and clouds run and the celestial sphere beyond perception of distance. Besides this, without going into details about the number of heavens, we can only note that the Bible refers to a third heaven (2 Cor.12:2), where the Apostle Paul says he knows a man who was caught up to the third heaven.

4. **What did God do on the third day of creation? Genesis 1:9-13 (Verdure, vegetation, trees of all kinds)**

"The earth brought forth vegetation, plants yielding seed according to their kinds, and trees bearing fruit."

- *It should be noted that, even before the creation of man, God prepared for him an ideal setting where, in contact with nature, he could continually flourish.*

5. **What did God do on the fourth day of creation? Genesis 1:14-19 (The sun, moon, stars)**

   "God made the two great lights—the greater light to rule the day and the lesser light to rule the night; he made the stars also."

   - *With the creation of the sun, it is the rising and setting of the sun that will biblically make the line of demarcation between day and night, between evening and morning. It is by convention that humanity (the Babylonians) will divide the day into a period of twenty-four (24) hours, 12 hours for the daytime period, and 12 hours for the night.*

6. **What did God do on the fifth day of creation? Genesis 1:20-23** (Living animals in the waters and the expanse of heaven)

   "God created the great sea creatures and every living creature that moves, with which the waters swarm... and every winged bird according to its kind. And God saw that it was good" v.21

7. **What did God do on the sixth day of creation? Genesis 1:24-31 (The animals living on the earth and man)**

   - The most spectacular realization of God during this sixth day is man: a masterpiece of creation, formed from the dust of the earth and the breath of life breathed into his nostrils. This is the origin of man, coming from the hands of the Creator. He is therefore not the result of a slow evolution extending over long periods of years, as Evolution claims. The second observation is that man was created in God's image, according to His likeness (Gen 1:26). This said, God is by nature good, just, and pure, man was in Eden with this original moral beauty.

   - According to Genesis 1:28, in commanding man to be fruitful and multiply, God thus established the basis for the reproduction of humanity, the principle according to which life can only come from life (biogenesis), which is opposite to abiogenesis which is defined as the appearance of life from inanimate matter.

- Moreover, God defines, in Eden, the dietary regime for mankind: a vegetarian diet. "And God said, Behold, I have given you every plant yielding seed that is on the face of all the earth, and every tree with seed in its fruit. You shall have them for food" Gen 1:29. This establishes that the original diet did not include the consumption of meat. It was necessary to wait long after the flood to see God permit man to consume it (Gen 9:5). This well meets the concerns of medical science which recognizes the superiority of the vegetarian diet over the meat diet.

8. What did God do on the seventh day of creation? Genesis 2:1,2 (God rested)

"Thus, the heavens and the earth were finished, and all their host (...) And on the seventh day, God finished the work that he had done, and he rested on the seventh day from all the work that he had done"

- *God did not work on the seventh day, he rested. It was for him a means of stopping and contemplating the creative work, and a means of indicating to a man who would have to work and get tired, the necessity of resting.*

9. What is one of the distinctive traits of the true God? Jeremiah 10:10-12 (Creator)

"He has made the earth by his power; He has established the world by his wisdom" v.12

- God alone created heaven, earth, and all that is in them.

10. By what power were all things brought into existence? Psalm 33:6,9

"By the word of the LORD the heavens were made, and by the breath of his mouth all their host... For he spoke, and it came to be; he commanded, and it stood firm."

- *God created everything by the "word". He did everything by a simple power of will. He speaks, and the thing happens. All this shows the greatness and magnificence of God.*

11. Having been created by God, to whom do we belong? 1 Cor. 6:19,20

"Do you not know that your body is a temple of the Holy Spirit within you, whom you have from God? You are not your own" v.19

- *Having been created by God, we belong to God; from these flows for us a great responsibility: that of obeying Him. There is no other way to recognize our belonging to and dependence on God.*

RECAP: THEMES FOR REFLECTION DRAWN FROM THIS STUDY:

1. The three (3) inconsistencies of the theory of Evolution.
2. Biogenesis and abiogenesis
3. The days of creation: literal or symbolic?
4. What did God do on the sixth and seventh days of creation?
5. The dietary regime given to man in Eden

STUDY #3: SIN

The book of Genesis teaches us that, in Eden, man was created in God's image, pure, just, and good. But, starting with the tragedy of Cain and Abel, we see that the social fabric is torn. The family, the basis of society is dislocated; men tear each other apart and it is with reason that one says that man has become a wolf to man. Nations clash in endless conflicts. In a word, God's image in man has been obliterated. What happened then?

Man's life on earth has become a calvary: diseases, physical and moral sufferings, death; whereas, in the Creator's intention, man was created for happiness and eternal happiness. Yes, something happened? An intruder got involved in the party at some point, and destroyed the relationships between the Creator and his creatures. Theologians are unanimous in qualifying it: sin. But what is sin? Where does it come from? and what then are its consequences for humanity? These are the questions that the present study proposes to answer.

1. What is sin? 1 John 3:4

"Whoever sins transgresses also the law: for sin is the transgression of the law."

- *The law is the rule, the norm, that expresses God's will towards humanity. Sin is the transgression of the law. It is the refusal of God; it is taking a direction opposite to that dictated by God. Sin is rebellion, revolt against God.*

2. In whom did sin originate? 1 John 3:8

"He who sins is of the devil, for the devil has sinned from the beginning" 1 John 3:8(a)

- *It is the devil who sinned for the first time and not Adam and Eve; but, he did it "from the beginning", at a time when our first parents were not yet created.*

3. Who is this devil? and how did sin first manifest itself? Ezekiel 28:14,15

"You were an anointed cherub that covers, and I had placed you so. You were upon the holy mountain of God; you walked up and down during the stones of fire... You were perfect in your ways from the day you were created, till iniquity was found in you"

- *Ezekiel, under the traits of the King of Tyre, describes an exceptional being, under the name "covering cherub" that theologians call: Lucifer. Lucifer which comes from Latin (lux, cis=light, ferre=carry) is translated as "light-bearer". This mighty angel, in heaven, was "perfect in his ways", and submitted to divine authority, until the day when iniquity took birth in his heart. Ezekiel 28:17(a), well indicates the form of this iniquity: "Your heart was lifted because of your beauty, you have corrupted your wisdom because of your brightness." Thus, pride was born in his heart which led him to revolt against divine authority and made him henceforth an angel in the service of evil: the devil, Satan, prince of darkness.*

4. What were the consequences of Lucifer's sin? Revelation 12:7-12 +

"And there was war in heaven: Michael and his angels fought against the dragon, and the dragon and his angels fought, but they did not prevail, neither was their place found any more in heaven (...) He was cast out into the earth, and his angels were cast out with him" v.7-9

- The consequences of Lucifer's sin (who became the devil) can be summarized thus:

  - a. *A war in heaven, between, on one hand, the angels faithful to God having at their head Michael (Jesus Christ), and, on the other hand, Lucifer (the devil), leading the angels in rebellion against God. Michael or Michaël, means, etymologically, "like God".*

  - b. *Lucifer and his angels are cast out of heaven to earth*

  - c. *The earth becomes henceforth the battlefield between God and Satan.*

- *"Sin originated in the heart of the one who, after Christ, had been most highly honored by God, the most powerful and glorious of all the inhabitants of Heaven. Before his fall, Lucifer was the first of the 'covering cherubs', holy and undefiled... Lucifer could have retained God's favor, loved, and honored by the angelic hosts, exercising his noble faculties to bless others and to glorify his Maker. But instead of seeking to exalt God and give him first place in the affection of his creatures, Lucifer sought to capture for himself their allegiance and homage. Coveting the honor that the Father had conferred on His Son, this prince of angels aspired to a power which Christ alone held the prerogative. In departing from this, Lucifer dishonored his Creator and brought ruin upon his head." (Ellen G White, The Great Controversy, pp.434-435, Inter-American Edition, 2012)*

5. How was sin introduced into the world? Gen 2:17; Gen 3:6

"But of the tree of the knowledge of good and evil, you shall not eat of it: for in the day that you eat thereof you shall surely die." Gen 2:17

"And when the woman saw that the tree was good for food and that it was pleasant to the eyes, and a tree to be desired to make one wise, she took of its fruit and did eat, and gave also unto her husband with her and he did eat." Gen 3:6

- In the passages above, two (2) expressions draw attention: "You shall not eat of the tree" and "She took of its fruit and did eat". Two (2) antagonistic or opposite expressions. One expresses the order, norm, or law of God, while the other expresses disobedience to this will or violation of this law. From then on, sin which began in heaven with Lucifer is introduced, henceforth into the world, our world, with all the consequences that will result.

6. What are the consequences of sin: for the serpent, the woman, and the man?

a. The serpent

"Upon your belly shall you go, and dust shall you eat all the days of your life... I will put enmity between you and the woman, between your seed and her seed; it shall bruise your head, and you shall bruise his heel," Gen 3:14(b),15.

- The serpent symbolizes here Satan, the devil, and the woman the Church. Genesis thus announces the cosmic conflict between good and evil, between God and Satan, between him and God's Church through the ages, and between Satan's offspring and that of the Church, Jesus. This prophecy announces not only the age-long struggle between God's Church and the Prince of Darkness but also the Church's victory over the Prince of Darkness.

b. The woman

"And unto the woman he said, I will greatly multiply your sorrow and your conception; in sorrow, you shall bring forth children; and your desire shall be to your husband, and he shall rule over you" Gen 3:16

- *If the concept "woman", in a prophetic sense can refer to the Church, in this passage it also refers to woman in her biological aspect. The two (2) main consequences or curses pronounced by the Creator against her area. Increase of suffering in pregnancy b. Husband's domination over woman.*

c. Man

"Cursed is the ground for your sake; in sorrow shall you eat of it all the days of your life. Thorns also and thistles shall it bring forth to you; and you shall eat the herb of the field (...) In the sweat of your face shall you eat bread, till you return unto the ground; for out of it were you taken: for dust you are, and unto dust shall you return" Gen 3:17(b),18,19

- *With sin and because of it, work for man becomes a calvary; it is in pain and suffering that he must earn his bread and death becomes inevitable. Sin has thus brought physical and moral suffering to humanity. Man has therefore lost his home, his life, and his happiness.*

7. To what extent do humans identify with sin?

"For all have sinned and fall short of the glory of God" Rom 3:23

"Therefore, just as through one man sin entered into the world, and death through sin, and thus death spread to all men because all sinned" Rom 5:12

- *All have sinned indiscriminately. The Bible does not recognize the idea that there would be a class of privileged people, born without sin or immaculate in conception. This theory which originated in a fringe of Christianity has no scriptural basis and, consequently, must be rejected.*

8. What is the final consequence of sin? James 1:15

"Then, when desire has conceived, it gives birth to sin; and sin, when it is full-grown, brings forth death"

- *Sin produces death. Sin, by introducing death into the world has blocked the Creator's plan for humanity, because man was created for eternal happiness. Death is not only this descent into the grave, when the breath of life has left our nostrils but also the final destruction, eternal death.*

9. Can man, without help, free himself from sin? Jeremiah 13:23

"Can the Ethiopian change his skin or the leopard its spots? Neither can you do good who are accustomed to doing evil"

- *The sinner cannot, alone, free himself from sin. Just as a drowning person needs an external hand to pull them from the water; the sinner too needs a savior. The Apostle Paul well described the desperate condition of sinful man in Romans 7: "For I have the desire to do what is good, but I cannot carry it out" v.18(b) "For I do not do the good I want to do, but the evil I do not want to do—this I keep on doing" v.19 "What a wretched man I am! Who will rescue me from this body that is subject to death?" v.24. Fortunately, Paul's cry which is that of mankind seems to have an answer: "Thanks be to God, who delivers me through Jesus Christ our Lord!" v.25*

10. What was the planned solution for man's salvation? Eph 1:4,5

"For he chose us in him before the creation of the world to be holy and blameless in his sight. In love, he predestined us for adoption to sonship through Jesus Christ, by his pleasure and will"

- *If God in His prescience and omniscience knew that our first parents would sin, He also, before the foundation of the world, elaborated a plan for man's salvation. However, despite this prescience, God could not prevent our first parents from sinning; because He created us with free will, this capacity to choose good or evil, obedience or disobedience.*

RECAP: THEMES FOR REFLECTION DRAWN FROM THIS STUDY

1. Definition of sin
2. The first manifestation of sin and its protagonist?
3. The introduction of sin into the world and its consequences for women and man
4. Can man, alone, free himself from sin?

STUDY #4: THE PLAN OF REDEMPTION

In Eden, God established for our first parents the conditions of life: obey. Put to a test, they failed; and consequently, death intervenes, eternal death. The Lord could have abandoned man to his fate because he had been warned, and God could have taken the universe as a witness. But He did not do it. He has, on the contrary, conceived a plan in favor of man: the plan of redemption. The word "redemption" comes from the Latin "redemption" which means ransom the fact of re-buying or buying again. Certainly, with sin, mankind was lost and delivered itself to the prince of darkness. To buy it again or redeem it, there is a price to pay. Who can satisfy this requirement?

The Bible teaches us that this conceived plan was planned before the foundation of the world. But what does this plan include? Who is at the center of this approach by God? The present study intends to answer these questions.

1. What does the plan of redemption imply? John 3:16

"For God so loved the world that he gave his one and only Son, that whoever believes in him shall not perish but have eternal life"

- *This plan comes down to the fact that God, to save humanity, accepts, through love, to give His Son, Jesus, so that all might be saved have eternal life. The word "whoever" well translates the universality of this plan which includes every person, regardless of their race, skin color, social and economic level, and origins. It is a total and complete salvation that includes mankind, without distinction. It is also the only condition for not perishing and having eternal life.*

2. **What nature did the Son of God take on when coming into the world? Philippians 2:5-8**

"Your attitude should be the same as that of Christ Jesus: Who, being in very nature God, did not consider equality with God something to be grasped, but made himself nothing, taking the very nature of a servant, being made in human likeness. And being found in appearance as a man, he humbled himself"

- *Man has sinned. To redeem him, a man must die in his place; but it must be a man without sin because the blood of a sinner has no value before God. The Bible declares that all have sinned and fall short of the glory of God (Rom 3:23). This constituted a dilemma for divinity. This is why Jesus, God, decided to become man to come die in man's place. (John 1:14). In a word, Jesus became man to save humanity.*

3. **What place does Jesus occupy in the plan of redemption?**

"For there is one God and one mediator between God and men, the man Christ Jesus" 1 Tim 2:5

"Salvation is found in no one else, for there is no other name under heaven given to men by which we must be saved" Acts 4:12

- *A mediator is defined as an intermediary, a facilitator, or a person who intervenes to facilitate an agreement between two or more persons. The one and only mediator between God and men is Jesus. He is the way, the truth, and the life (John 14:6); Jesus is not one among several mediators. The Bible does not recognize the idea that exceptional beings exercise in heaven, beside the Father, a ministry of intercession in favor of humans. Those whom the Bible calls "Saints" have all been redeemed and saved in the same way by the blood of Jesus. There is salvation in no other, no other name by which we can be saved: Jesus.*

4. What must be done to accept this salvation?

a. Confess one's sins 1 John 1:9

"If we confess our sins, he is faithful and just and will forgive us our sins and purify us from all unrighteousness"

- *To confess is to recognize one's sins, to admit them to God and implore His pardon. This is the first step to approach God. One who does not recognize their fault cannot approach God. The Psalmist David said: "For I acknowledge my transgressions, and my sin is always before me." Psalm 51:5; "Against you, you only, have I sinned and done what is evil in your sight." Psalm 51:6(a).*

- *David confessed his sins and confessed directly to God. This is what Ezra declares: "Now therefore make confession to the Lord God of your fathers and do his will" Ezra 10:11(a). This is the rule. When we recognize our sins, alone, in a face to face with God, we confess our fault and implore His pardon "in Jesus' name". Contrary to this, church leaders unfortunately introduced into religious practices, at the fourth Lateran Council in 1215, what is called "auricular confession", a practice according to which a person presents themselves before a church leader to confess their sins to them. And the latter says they grant pardon or "absolution" to the sinner. Considering God's Word and precisely the plan of redemption, this constitutes an impediment to Christ's priestly ministry.*

b. Repent: Acts 3:19

"Repent, then, and turn to God, so that your sins may be wiped out"

- *To accept this salvation offered by Jesus, it is not enough to confess or admit one's fault, one must repent. Repentance is feeling regret regarding the sin committed and the resolution or decision to abandon it.*

- *"Whoever conceals their sins does not prosper, but the one who confesses and renounces them finds mercy" Prov 28:13*

c. *Obey*: Matthew 7:21

"Not everyone who says to me, 'Lord, Lord,' will enter the kingdom of heaven, but only the one who does the will of my Father who is in heaven"

- *Being registered in church records and being faithful to cultic practices cannot in any way ensure salvation; but only sincere obedience to God's will.*

5. What does Jesus teach about the importance of conversion? Matt 18:3

"And he said: 'Truly I tell you, unless you change and become like little children, you will never enter the kingdom of heaven'"

- *This declaration of Jesus implies two (2) concepts: conversion and humility. Conversion is being transformed, and changed. Following Christ necessarily implies giving one's life a new orientation, and having a new way of living. Humility is being like children. Being humble is being attentive and receptive to God's orders.*

6. What transformation is implied in conversion? Ezekiel 36:26

"I will give you a new heart and put a new spirit in you; I will remove from you your heart of stone and give you a heart of flesh."

- *This transformation henceforth implies a heart of flesh, a heart sensitive to the influence of the Holy Spirit, according to what is written: "Today, if you hear his voice, do not harden your hearts as you did in the rebellion, during the time of testing in the wilderness" Heb 3:7,8*

7. What assurance does the sinner receive in the framework of the redemption plan? Isaiah 1:18

" Come now, let us settle the matter,' says the LORD. 'Though your sins are like scarlet, they shall be as white as snow; though they are red as crimson, they shall be like wool.'"

- *The pardon that God offers us is total and complete. It is this assurance that encourages us to approach him, whatever our spiritual state and our past.*

8. **What are the excuses commonly invoked when refusing to respond to the Lord's call? Luke 14:16-20**

• *Like those invited to this feast, one always gives excuses or pretexts for not responding to Jesus' call. Thus, one lets pass the time or opportunity to make the greatest decision, that of being saved.*

RECAP: THEMES FOR REFLECTION DRAWN FROM THIS STUDY:

1. Jesus' role in the redemption plan

2. What do the concepts imply: confession, repentance, obedience?

3. How many mediators are there between God and men?

4. Explain the word "mediator"

STUDY #5: WHO IS JESUS?

Who is Jesus? Pertinent question. For some, Jesus is an important character, because he divided the history of humanity in two; for others, Jesus is a prophet like Moses, Mohammed, and Buddha. In certain Christian religions, Jesus is the Son of God, but not God. If they accept him as such, he is, however, an inferior God compared to the divinity of the Father. It must be recognized that, like in today's world, Jesus' contemporaries, his disciples, could not often identify him correctly or had an erroneous opinion about his identity. All this makes the present study of great importance.

1. **How did Jesus' disciples identify him? Matthew 16:13-16**

"'Who do people say the Son of Man is?' They replied, 'Some say John the Baptist; others say Elijah; and still others, Jeremiah or one of the prophets.' 'But what about you?' he asked. 'Who do you say I am?' Simon Peter answered, 'You are the Messiah, the Son of the living God.'"

• *Even in Jesus' entourage their reigned confusion about his identity (John the Baptist, Elijah, or Jeremiah). Today's world runs the same danger, the same risk; because before developing such a relationship with Jesus, one must first know who he is. Fortunately, Peter gave the good and right answer: "You are the Christ, the Son of the living God"*

2. What makes Jesus an exceptional being? His exceptional birth: Luke 1:34,35; Luke 2:6,7

"How will this be, Mary asked the angel since I am a virgin?"... "So, the holy one to be born will be called the Son of God" Luke 1:34,35

"While they were there, the time came for the baby to be born" Luke 2:6

- *Medical science recognizes that for conception of a human being to occur, there must be the meeting of a male cell (sperm) with an ovum. Jesus' conception defied this rule: "The power of the Most High will overshadow you." Jesus' conception and coming from a woman make him an exceptional being, having a dual nature: God and Man. Jesus' divine-human nature offers humanity very great advantages: As God, he knows God's affairs; and as man, he knows human nature and weakness. As such, he can easily build the bridge between the two, and reconcile Divinity and humanity.*

3. What attributes of Jesus establish his Divinity?

a. Jesus, Creator: John 1:3; Col 1:16,17

"All things were created through him and for him" Col 1:16

- *Jesus, as the second person of divinity participated in the creative work. Creation is one of the characteristic attributes of divinity. Only God has created and only God can create.*

b. **Jesus, Omnipresent**: Matt 28:20; Matt 18:20

"And surely I am with you always, to the very end of the age"

"For where two or three gather in my name, there am I with them"

- *By making these declarations, Jesus affirms his omnipresence. We are never alone, even in the darkest circumstances of life.*

c. **Jesus, Omnipotent**: Matt 28:18

"All authority in heaven and on earth has been given to me"

- *If Satan is powerful, God is All-powerful. Jesus affirms here his Omnipotence. By trusting in him, the forces of evil cannot reach you, because you remain in the shadow of the Almighty.*

d. *Jesus*, **Omniscient**: Col 2:3

"In whom have hidden all the treasures of wisdom and knowledge"

e. **Jesus, Immutable**: Heb 13:8

"Jesus Christ is the same yesterday and today and forever"

- *Jesus does not change, as God has declared "I will not violate my covenant or alter what my lips have uttered" Ps 89:35*

f. *Jesus*, **forgiving sins**: Mark 2:5-7

"*When Jesus saw their faith, he said to the paralyzed man, 'Son, your sins are forgiven.' (...) 'He's blaspheming! Who can forgive sins but God alone?'*"

g. *Jesus*, **claiming the same title as his Father**: Isaiah 44:6; Rev 22:13

"I am the Alpha and the Omega, the First and the Last, the Beginning and the End" Rev 22:13

h. **Jesus, his divinity attested**: Rom 9:5

"Christ, who is God over all, forever praised! Amen"

4. As representative of humanity, what function does Jesus fulfill with the Father?

- Advocate: 1 John 2:1-2

"If anybody does sin, we have an advocate with the Father—Jesus Christ, the Righteous One"

5. is Jesus interested in our immediate human needs besides our eternal salvation?

a. **Jesus, the great physician:** Mark 5:35

"But Jesus told her, 'Daughter, your faith has healed you. Go in peace and be freed from your suffering.'"

- *Just as Jesus healed this woman who had been suffering from bleeding for twelve (12) years, he still heals today. Whatever the illness or suffering, the last word has not been said if Jesus has not yet pronounced it.*

b. *Jesus*, **the great provider: Matt** 14:15-21

"Jesus replied, 'They do not need to go away. You give them something to eat... He broke the loaves and gave them to the disciples, who distributed them to the people"

- *Jesus is not insensitive to our human material needs: hunger, nakedness, physical and moral sufferings. This miracle of the multiplication of loaves where he fed a hungry crowd means that he can still be attentive to our pressing needs today. Trust in him. Jesus is not only a God who is interested in our future eternal life, but he is also present in our daily life; in a word, Jesus is all in all.*

RECAP: THEMES FOR REFLECTION DRAWN FROM THIS STUDY:

1. What makes us say that Jesus is both God and Man?
2. Recall the divine attributes of Jesus
3. Jesus and our immediate human needs
4. Jesus' function with the Father

STUDY #6: JESUS AND PROPHECY

In some people's opinion, the Old Testament of the Bible is outdated, outmoded, and should be shelved. For them, the teachings contained therein and which were written before Jesus are expired. That said, only the New Testament counts and Jesus is present only in the New Testament the Christian dispensation. However, an in-depth study reveals the unity of God's Word, which is presented in two parts: the Old and New Testament. They form a harmonious whole; one explains the other. The second reveals, on many occasions, the fulfillment of prophecies announced in the first, and more specifically those relating to Jesus.

A biblical prophecy is a message given by a prophet and which has been communicated to him by God. This message generally implies the revelation of divine will relative either to the era in which he lives, or to events to come. The present study will allow us to:

    a. identifies the prophecies relating to Jesus, announced in the Old Testament, and fulfilled in the New.

    b. strengthens the conviction that the teachings of the two Testaments represent a single letter addressed by God to all humanity.

1. According to the Bible, what importance should be given to prophecy? 2 Peter 1:19

"And we have the prophetic message more fully confirmed. You will do well to pay attention to this as to a lamp shining in a dark place until the day dawns and the morning star rises in your hearts"

- *God reveals to us, through the prophets, not only His teachings or His will for the present moment, but also for the future. The apostle exhorts us to pay attention to it and to be interested in the study of prophecy. However, it should be noted that the Word of God indicates that, outside of the prophets noted in the biblical canon, God would pour out His Spirit on others in the last days: "In the last days, God says, I will pour out my Spirit on all people. Your sons and daughters will prophesy, your young men will see visions, your old men will dream dreams." Acts 2:17*

2. What shows that Jesus is present throughout all of Scripture? Luke 24:27, 44

"And beginning with Moses and all the Prophets, he explained to them what was said in all the Scriptures concerning himself." v.27

"(...) Everything must be fulfilled that is written about me in the Law of Moses, the Prophets and the Psalms." v.44

- Jesus affirms, through these declarations, that He is present in all Scripture, that is, throughout the writings of the Old Testament prophets. Moreover, it should be emphasized that when Jesus says "in all the Scriptures", He specifically refers to the Old Testament; because at the time of Jesus, the New Testament had not yet been written. It would be until the end of the first century to see the completion of the writing of this second part of the Bible.

3. What are the prophecies relating to Jesus, announced in the Old Testament, and fulfilled in the New?

a. Victory over Satan and death: OT: Gen 3:15; NT: 1 Cor 15:25, 26

"And I will put enmity between you and the woman, and between your offspring and hers; he will crush your head, and you will strike his heel." Gen 3:15

"For he must reign until he has put all his enemies under his feet. The last enemy to be destroyed is death." 1 Cor 15:25, 26

- *The woman of Gen 3:15 refers not only to Eve as a physical person, but also symbolically to the Church. The concept "woman" always symbolizes the Church in biblical prophecy: the submissive woman, faithful wife, is the Church or people of God throughout the ages and the unfaithful woman or prostitute is the Church that has denied its first love, the teaching of God's Word. The Apostle John, in the book of Revelation, identifies the first as "a woman clothed with the sun" (Rev 12:1) and the second as "the great prostitute" (Rev 17:1).*

- *God's Church or people of God throughout the Bible is the line of men and women who serve God. This line passes through Shem (Noah's descendant), Abraham, Jacob (Israel), Judah, David, up to Jesus. The Apostle Paul, in the book of Galatians, identifies Jesus as Abraham's seed and certainly, through Abraham, to the seed of the woman (Church). "And if you belong to Christ, then you are Abraham's seed, and heirs according to the promise." Gal 3:29. "Now to Abraham and his seed were the promises made. He saith not, and to seeds, as of many; but as of one, and to thy seed, which is Christ." Gal 3:16*

- *Gen 3:15 announces the cosmic conflict between God and Satan, between Satan's seed and the Church. But it also announced at the same time the Church's victory over Satan, with Jesus's death and resurrection. Jesus's sufferings in the context of His passion represent healing wounds compared to the great victory of the cross.*

b. His birthplace: OT: Micah 5:2; NT: Luke 2:4, 6

"But you, Bethlehem Ephrathah, though you are small among the clans of Judah, out of you will come for me one who will be ruler over Israel." Micah 5:2(a)

"So, Joseph also went up from the town of Nazareth in Galilee to Judea, to Bethlehem the town of David." Luke 2:4(a)

- *Jesus's birth happened in Bethlehem, as announced by the prophet Micah.*

c. His passion (His sufferings): OT Isaiah 53:4, 5; NT: Acts 5:30

"Surely he took up our pain and bore our suffering... But he was pierced for our transgressions, he was crushed for our iniquities; the punishment that brought us peace was on him." Isaiah 53:4, 5

"The God of our ancestors raised Jesus from the dead—whom you killed by hanging him on a cross." Acts 5:30

- *Theologians unanimously affirm that Isaiah is the most messianic prophet of the Bible or even the prophet of the Gospel. He prophesied about Jesus more than any other. He describes in detail the scenes surrounding Jesus's suffering and death.*

d. *His* eternal origin: OT: Micah 5:2(b); NT: John 8:58

"Out of you will come for me one who will be ruler over Israel, whose origins are from of old, from ancient times." Micah 5:2(b)

"Very truly I tell you," Jesus answered, "before Abraham was born, I am!"

- Jesus as God and Creator existed before Abraham. Micah announced it thus.

e. His Divinity foretold: OT: Isaiah 9:6; NT: 1 John 5:20

"For to us a child is born, to us a son is given, and the government will be on his shoulders. And he will be called Wonderful Counselor, Mighty God, Everlasting Father, Prince of Peace." Isaiah 9:6

"We know also that the Son of God has come… He is the true God and eternal life." 1 John 5:20

- Isaiah announced, hundreds of years before Jesus's birth, that He is God.

f. Casting lots for His garments: OT: Psalm 22:18; NT: Matt 27:35

"They divide my clothes among them and cast lots for my garment." Ps 22:18

"When they had crucified him, they divided up his clothes by casting lots." Matt 27:35

g. His tomb among the rich: OT: Isaiah 53:9; NT: Matt 27:57, 60(a)

"He was assigned a grave with the wicked, and with the rich in his death." Isaiah 53:9

"As evening approached, there came a rich man from Arimathea, named Joseph, who had himself become a disciple of Jesus… and placed it in his new tomb that he had cut out of the rock." Matt 27:57, 60(a)

h. His resurrection foretold: OT: Ps 16:10; NT: Acts 2:24

"Because you will not abandon me to the realm of the dead, nor will you let your faithful one see decay." Ps 16:10

"But God raised him from the dead, freeing him from the agony of death, because death couldn't keep its hold on him." Acts 2:24

Jesus's Victory over sin and death lies not only in His death on the cross but especially in His resurrection.

"And if Christ has not been raised, our preaching is useless and so is your faith." 1 Cor 15:14

i. Co-regency with His Father: OT: Ps 110:1; NT: Heb 1:13

"The Lord says to my lord: 'Sit at my right hand until I make your enemies a footstool for your feet.'" Ps 110:1

"To which of the angels did God ever say, 'Sit at my right hand until I make your enemies a footstool for your feet'?" Heb 1:13

RECAP: REFLECTION THEMES DRAWN FROM THIS STUDY:

1. Definition of prophecy and its importance
2. Jesus and the Old Testament
3. Which Old Testament prophet spoke the most about Jesus?
4. Name some prophecies about Jesus announced in the Old Testament and fulfilled in the New.

STUDY #7: JESUS IS COMING

We suffer and we die; yet man was created for a future of happiness. The Bible teaches us that sin, by entering the world, also introduces the series of evils that we know. Jesus came and brought, through His death on the cross, an answer to sin and death. But Jesus lived for a time on earth and did not stay; He ascended to heaven. Should He stay there permanently? What does the Bible say? Is the doctrine of Jesus's return an invention of Christian religions or a biblical doctrine? And if Jesus must return, why? How? And with what consequences? These are the questions that will be addressed in this study.

1. **What promise did Jesus make to His disciples about His return? John 14:1-3**

"**And** if I go and prepare a place for you, I will come back and take you to be with me that you also may be where I am." v.3

- "**I will come back**" **is** Jesus's affirmation. This is what gives all authority to this doctrine through the ages. Men generally do not keep their word; they say something today and deny it tomorrow. This is the instability that characterizes man. But here, it is Jesus Himself who says it; Christians believe it and have lived for centuries with the hope of this return.

2. **How has this promise sustained God's people through the ages? Job 19:25-27; Philippians 3:20, 21**

"But our citizenship is in heaven. And we eagerly await a Savior from there, the Lord Jesus Christ, who, by the power that enables him to bring everything under his control, will transform our lowly bodies so that they will be like his glorious body." Phil 3:20, 21

The promise of Jesus's return has sustained and strengthened the faith of God's servants. Even Job who lived long before Jesus came to earth, contemplated by faith the hope of this return and declared: "My eyes will see him." For the Apostle Paul: "We await the Lord Jesus Christ who will transform our lowly bodies."

This sin-withered body will be restored to its original beauty.

3. **What is the message found in Jesus's final revelation: Rev 22:12, 20**

"**Lo**ok, I am coming soon! My reward is with me, and I will give to each person according to what they have done." v.12

- *"I am coming soon" is Jesus's affirmation.*

4. Why is Jesus returning?

a. He comes to get His people: John 14:2,3; 1 Thess 4:16

"I will take you to be with me that you also may be where I am." John 14:3(b)

b. Mortality changed to immortality: 1 Cor 15:51-53

"The trumpet will sound, and the dead will be raised imperishable, and we will be changed. For the perishable must clothe itself with the imperishable, and the mortal with immortality." 1 Cor 15:52(b), 53

c. He comes to judge the world: 2 Tim 4:1

"In the presence of God and of Christ Jesus, who will judge the living and the dead, and given his appearing and his kingdom..."

d. He will bring the reward with Him: Heb 9:28

"So Christ was sacrificed once to take away the sins of many; and he will appear a second time, not to bear sin, but to bring salvation to those who are waiting for him."

- *Jesus returns not only to give to each according to what they have done but especially to reward those who wait for Him for their salvation. Waiting for Jesus means obeying His will and that of His Father.*

e. *He will destroy the wicked: 2 Thess 1:7, 8*

"And give relief to you who are troubled, and to us as well. This will happen when the Lord Jesus is revealed from heaven in blazing fire with his powerful angels. He will punish those who do not know God and do not obey the gospel of our Lord Jesus."

- *The wicked is not necessarily one who commits crimes. According to the Bible, the wicked is any person who does not obey the gospel of our Lord Jesus.*

f. *He will reign eternally: Heb 1:8*

"But about the Son he says, 'Your throne, O God, will last forever and ever; a scepter of justice will be the scepter of your kingdom.'"

5. How will Jesus return? Acts 1:10, 11; Matt 24:27, 30

"This same Jesus, who has been taken from you into heaven, will come back in the same way you have seen him go into heaven." Acts 1:11(b)

"For as lightning that comes from the east is visible even in the west, so will be the coming of the Son of Man... Then all the peoples of the earth will mourn when they see the Son of Man coming on the clouds of heaven, with power and great glory." Matt 24:27, 30(b)

- *Jesus's coming will be visible, spectacular, and glorious. It will be as visible as His ascension was. The opinion that this coming will be discreet, secret, symbolic, has no scriptural basis, and must be rejected by all who accept God's Word as the basis of their faith.*

6. When will Jesus return? Matt 24:36, 42-44

"But about that day or hour, no one knows, not even the angels in heaven, nor the Son, but only the Father." Matt 24:36

"Therefore, keep watch, because you do not know on what day your Lord will come... So you also must be ready, because the Son of Man will come at an hour when you do not expect him." Matt 24:42, 44

- *No one knows either the date or the hour of Jesus's return. God wanted it this way. Throughout human history, people have tried in vain to predict dates for the end of the world or Jesus's return. The Bible is clear on this subject - no one knows.*

7. What should we do while waiting for this return? 1 John 3:3; Luke 21:34-36

"All who have this hope in him purify themselves, just as he is pure." 1 John 3:3

- *To prepare for Jesus's return is to purify ourselves as He is pure: it is to obey or submit to His will.*

RECAP: REFLECTION THEMES DRAWN FROM THIS STUDY:

1. Is Jesus's returning a biblical doctrine?
2. List some reasons justifying Jesus's return.
3. How will Jesus return?
4. When will Jesus return?

STUDY #8: SIGNS OF JESUS'S RETURN

No one knows either the day or date of Jesus's return: this is the great truth. Therefore, those who say otherwise or who claim to advance dates concerning the end of the world or Jesus's return do so outside of God's Word. However, the Bible teaches us that God never wants to surprise us or catch us off guard. He always sends warnings. He did it in the case of the flood, in Noah's time. He sent warnings to Lot before the destruction of Sodom and Gomorrah. And regarding Jesus's return, He also sends warnings or signs to humanity through the Bible from which we can recognize whether this event is near, and prepare accordingly.

It seems these signs touch several domains. Since Jesus lived on earth, this reality preoccupied the disciples; they asked Him questions about it and these questions still interest us today. What is the Bible's answer on this subject? Are there really signs announcing Jesus's return?

1. **What question did the disciples ask Jesus about the end of the world? Matt 24:3**

"Tell us when will this happen, and what will be the sign of your coming and of the end of the age?

The question of the disciples consists of two parts:

   a. Their concern about the destruction of Jerusalem, which occurred in the year 70 AD with the invasion of the Roman army.

   b. The signs of the return of Jesus.

2. How can we know that the end is near? Matt 24:32, 33

"Now learn this lesson from the fig tree: As soon as its twigs get tender and its leaves come out, you know that summer is near. Even so, when you see all these things, you know that He is near, right at the door."

- *This declaration by Jesus indicates that the Bible contains markers, signposts showing the proximity of Jesus's return, that is, "the Son of Man is near, at the door." These signs should concern several aspects of life.*

3. In what conditions should the world find itself in the last days?

a. Endless wars: Matt 24:6, 7

"You will hear of wars and rumors of wars: see that you are not alarmed, for this must take place, but the end is not yet. Nation will rise against nation, and kingdom against kingdom."

- *Since World War I in 1914, the world has been transformed into a real battlefield. We still remember that during World War II (August 6 and 9, 1945), atomic bombings by American troops on Hiroshima and Nagasaki (Japanese cities) killed between 150,000 and 250,000 people. Conflicts: Iran-Iraq, Israel-Palestine, United States-Russia, raise serious concerns about humanity's future. Increasingly deadly weapons are being invented. Peace agreements initiated and concluded throughout the world under the authority of the United Nations (UN) have not had satisfactory results.*

- *All of this relates to biblical prophecy: "While people are saying, 'Peace and safety,' destruction will come on them suddenly, as labor pains on a pregnant woman, and they will not escape." 1 Thess 5:3*

b. Moral Conditions: Widespread carelessness: Matt 24:37-39

"As it was in the days of Noah, so it will be at the coming of the Son of Man... For in the days before the flood, people were eating and drinking, marrying, and giving in marriage, up to the day Noah entered the ark; they knew nothing about what would happen until the flood came and took them all away. That is how it will be at the coming of the Son of Man."

- *The same carelessness that characterized the antediluvian world is found in today's world. People are occupied with everything: frenzied pursuit of money, pleasures, satisfaction of material needs, but no place for God and eternal life. This is a sign of the times. Just as the flood surprised the antediluvians, so it will be at Jesus's next return.*

c. *Moral* degeneration: 2 Tim 3:1-5

"But mark this: There will be terrible times in the last days. People will be lovers of themselves, lovers of money... lovers of pleasure rather than lovers of God."

- *This is thus the description of the times of the last days predicted by the Bible. We can thus understand that we are effectively living in the final moments of this world's history.*

d. Growing iniquity: Matt 24:12

"Because of the increase of wickedness, the love of most will grow cold."

4. Is the attitude of mockers a sign of the times? 2 Peter 3:3, 4

"Above all, you must understand that in the last days scoffers will come, scoffing and following their own evil desires. They will say, 'Where is this "coming" he promised? Ever since our ancestors died, everything goes on as it has since the beginning of creation.'"

- *The attitude of mockers toward Jesus's return can greatly resemble that of the antediluvians for whom the announcement of a flood seemed utopian and senseless at a time when it had not yet rained.*

5. What are the other signs related to Jesus's return? James 5:4, 6, 8

"Look! The wages you failed to pay the workers who mowed your fields are crying out against you. The cries of the harvesters have reached the ears of the Lord Almighty. You have condemned and murdered the innocent one, who was not opposing you... Be patient, for the Lord's coming is near."

These passages point out certain practices that will prevail before Jesus's coming:

- Ill-gotten wealth
- Social injustices
- Indifference to others' misfortunes

6. What should we do consider these signs being fulfilled? Matt 24:44

"So, you also must be ready, because the Son of Man will come at an hour when you do not expect him."

- *The most solemn exhortation is to be ready, that is, to obey God's will as expressed in His Holy Word.*

7. Is Jesus delaying His coming? 2 Peter 3:9

"The Lord is not slow in keeping his promise, as some understand slowness. Instead, he is patient with you, not wanting anyone to perish, but everyone to come to repentance."

- *Jesus is patient with us; but this patience will not last forever. Just as one day the door of the ark was closed, one day the door of grace will close. The events unfolding around us each day well characterize a world in crisis and announce the end times. This crisis has multiple dimensions: political, social, economic... The proliferation of nuclear weapons among the great power's casts over our world the specter of a worldwide confrontation that risks annihilating our civilization. Respect for law is disappearing. Crime appears as an ever-present danger threatening the existence of organized society.*

It is the end of morality. We are already living in the time of the great famines announced for the end of history. These signs deliver us a message; it is the end times. Jesus is coming soon.

RECAP: REFLECTION THEMES DRAWN FROM THIS STUDY:

1. Does the Bible Anticipate Signs Announcing Jesus's Return?

2. What signs?

    a. In the political world

    b. In society

    c. The mockers

3. Is Jesus delaying?

4. What attitude should we have regarding this return?

STUDY #9: JESUS'S MEDIATORIAL WORK

A mediator is one who is placed between two persons or parties to bring them together, reconcile them - an intermediary. Sin in Eden broke the relationship between the Creator and man; and the wages of sin is death (Rom 6:23). But throughout the ages, God has always been concerned with bringing us closer to Him through a system of mediation.

During the Old Testament period, God established the system: The sanctuary with its two compartments (the holy place and the most holy place), the priests with the high priest at their head; the rites according to which the services should be conducted. The priests attached to sanctuary services were recruited exclusively from among members of the tribe of Levi. And it was through their ministry that repentant sinners approached God to obtain forgiveness of their sins. All this constituted the Levitical priestly system based on the immolation of animals and the shedding of blood. But was this system meant to last perpetually or be replaced by others? How did it function? What characterizes mediation in the Christian era?

1. **What general principle did God establish for the forgiveness of sins? Prov 28:13; Isaiah 1:18**

"**Whoe**ver conceals their sins does not prosper, but the one who confesses and renounces them finds mercy." Prov 28:13

The path laid out by God for us to receive His forgiveness is:

- Recognize our sins

- Confess them
- Forsake them

2. **What did the sinner do to obtain forgiveness before Jesus's coming? Lev 4:3, 13-14, 27-28, 32-33, 35(b)**

"If you offer a lamb, you must present a female without defect." Lev 4:32

"In this way the priest will make atonement for them for the sin they have committed, and they will be forgiven." Lev 4:35(b)

- *In this Levitical priesthood, daily, as people sinned, according to the sinner's status (priest, leader, community member), an animal had to be sacrificed and blood sprinkled on the altar. Thus, by confessing their sins and through the priest's ministry, the sinner approached the Lord to obtain forgiveness of their sins.*

3. **After the accumulation of sins during a year, what did the high priest do on the tenth day of the seventh month? Lev 16:29-30, 34; Heb 9:6, 7**

"**This is** to be a lasting ordinance for you: On the tenth day of the seventh month, you must deny yourselves and not do any work... because on this day atonement will be made for you, to cleanse you. Then, before the Lord, you will be clean from all your sins." Lev 16:29, 30

"The priests entered regularly into the outer room to carry on their ministry. But only the high priest entered the inner room, and that only once a year, and never without blood, which he offered for himself and for the sins the people had committed in ignorance." Heb 9:6, 7

- *Once a year, on the 10th day of the seventh month, comes the great Day of Atonement, also called the day of great pardon, the "Yom Kippur". On this day, the High Priest enters the Most Holy Place of the sanctuary (the second part), to offer for himself and the people a general atonement for all sins committed in Israel during the year. Thus, symbolically, the sanctuary was purified and cleared of all sins accumulated during the year on the altar: it was a day of deliverance.*

4. When did the earthly sanctuary services lose their value? Matt 27:50, 51

"And Jesus cried out again with a loud voice and yielded up his spirit. And behold, the curtain of the temple was torn in two, from top to bottom, and the earth shook, and the rocks were split."

- *Jesus's death on the cross ended the Levitical priesthood. The true Lamb of God was sacrificed; henceforth, it is no longer the blood of animals that provides forgiveness to the sinner, but that of Jesus. The antitype has replaced the type. The blood of bulls and goats prefigured and announced Jesus's blood which, long after, was to flow on the cross. This is indeed what the Apostle Paul declares: "For it is impossible for the blood of bulls and goats to take away sins. Therefore, when Christ came into the world, he said: 'Sacrifice and offering you did not desire, but a body you prepared for me.'" Heb 10:4, 5*

5. Where does Jesus exercise His mediatorial work? Heb 9:24

"For Christ did not enter a sanctuary made with human hands that was only a copy of the true one; he entered heaven itself, now to appear for us in God's presence."

- *Jesus exercises His priestly ministry in heaven, beside the Father. Each time we sin and confess our sins in His name, He presents His pierced hands to the Father and claims His pardon on our behalf, in the name of that shed blood.*

6. With what assurance can the sinner approach Jesus? Heb 4:14, 16

"Let us then approach God's throne of grace with confidence, so that we may receive mercy and find grace to help us in our time of need." Heb 4:16

- *Whatever our spiritual state, we can have the assurance that He will accept us.*

7. ***Will* Jesus intercede forever? Heb 9:28; Rev 22:11, 12**

"So Christ was sacrificed once to take away the sins of many; and he will appear a second time, not to bear sin, but to bring salvation to those who are waiting for him." Heb 9:28

- *Jesus will not intercede forever. Soon, He will lay aside His advocate's robes to put on those of the judge. Then, the door of grace will be closed and the fate of sinners sealed; as before the flood, at a certain point, the door of the ark was closed.*

8. **What warning is given to those living in the last days? Acts 17:30, 31**

"In the past God overlooked such ignorance, but now he commands all people everywhere to repent. For he has set a day when he will judge the world with justice by the man he has appointed. He has given proof of this to everyone by raising him from the dead."

- *God now commands all people everywhere to repent: this is the present truth.*

9. **What exhortation is made to all who receive knowledge of God's Word? Heb 10:26, 27**

"**If** we deliberately keep on sinning after we have received the knowledge of the truth, no sacrifice for sins is left, but only a fearful expectation of judgment and of raging fire that will consume the enemies of God."

10. **What is the ultimate exhortation to those who hear God's voice? Heb 3:7, 8**

"So, as the Holy Spirit says: 'Today, if you hear his voice, do not harden your hearts as you did in the rebellion, during the time of testing in the wilderness.'"

- *God invites us not to close our hearts to the Holy Spirit's influence if we hear His voice speaking to us.*

RECAP: REFLECTION THEMES DRAWN FROM THIS STUDY:

1. **What** was the Levitical priesthood?
2. From which tribe were the priests in Israel recruited?
3. What did the repentant sinner do in this system?
4. When did the earthly sanctuary services end?
5. Where does Jesus exercise His mediatorial work?
6. Will Jesus exercise this work eternally?

STUDY #10: THE LAW OF GOD

Law in general is the regulator of human life in society. What would happen if the laws governing Earth's movements (rotation and revolution) were to disappear? One face of the Earth would be continuously illuminated by the sun and the other in darkness. What would happen if a country was not governed by laws? The social order would be dislocated: there would be no duties and rights of citizens toward each other; no duties toward the State. Even automobile traffic could not function without law; pedestrians would be the main victims.

If humans, as bad as they are, recognize the necessity of laws, would not God who is Wisdom itself also have laws that are the basis of His government? Yes, the Bible affirms that God has a law. However, it must be specified that God's law in Holy Scripture appears in different categories or forms. It can refer to:

1. **The Torah:** (etymologically: Hebrew: torah "instruction"; Greek: nomos "law").

It is all of God's teaching transmitted to Moses through the five books (the Pentateuch) and addressed to Israel. It is placed indifferently in the Bible under the names: The Law, the Law of Moses, the Book of the Law, the Book of the Law of Moses, the Book of the Law of God (Nehemiah 8:1-8; 1 Kings 2:3)

2. **The Decalogue or Ten Commandments,** called by theologians "moral law" (Exodus 20:1-17; Deuteronomy 5:1-22).

3. **The ceremonial laws:** including rules and norms related to the Levitical priestly system and the rites that were attached to the Old Covenant of the Old Testament. (Exodus 25-30, 35-40; Leviticus 1-10, 12-17, 21-25)

4. **Israel's judicial system**: including civil and criminal laws that regulated this people's life within the framework of Theocracy. (Exodus 21-23; Leviticus 18-20; Deut.15, 19-26)

5. **Health laws:** including divine instructions related to diet. (Leviticus 11; Deut.14:1-21)

- It is the moral law or Ten Commandments that is the object of our attention in this study.

1. **What did God give Moses on Mount Sinai and what is its content? Exodus 31:18; Exodus 20:1-17**

"When the Lord finished speaking to Moses on Mount Sinai, he gave him the two tablets of the covenant law, the tablets of stone inscribed by the finger of God." Deut 31:18

- The word decalogue comes from Greek (deca: ten and logos: discourse). These are the ten commandments written by God Himself on two stone tablets and given to Moses. This is the only text of God's Word written "by the finger of God." All other parts of the Bible are written by prophets, certainly inspired by God. This is indeed what indicates the value of this document: a text addressed by God Himself to Israel and to all humanity.

The content of this text (Exodus 20:1-17) is presented as follows:

- **First commandment (v.3)** "You shall have no other gods before me"

- **2nd commandment (v.4)** "You shall not make for yourself an image in the form of anything"

- **3rd commandment (v.7)** "You shall not misuse the name of the Lord your God"

- **4th commandment (v.8)** "Remember the Sabbath day by keeping it holy"

- **5th commandment (v.12)** "Honor your father and your mother"

- **6th commandment (v.13)** "You shall not murder"

- **7th commandment (v.14)** "You shall not commit adultery"

- **8th commandment (v.15)** "You shall not steal"

- **9th commandment (v.16)** "You shall not give false testimony against your neighbor

- **10th commandment (v.17)** "You shall not covet your neighbor's house, nor his wife, nor anything that belongs to your neighbor"

2. What are the characteristics of this law?

a. It is moral:

- *It establishes moral principles and is the basis of all human legislation that aims to be moral. It is the basis of family and society stability. There is no nation on earth that can establish rules contrary to the decalogue in their civil and criminal codes without being immoral.*

b. It is a condensed or summary of love: Matt 22:36-40

"Teacher, which is the greatest commandment in the Law? Jesus replied: 'Love the Lord your God with all your heart and with all your soul and with all your mind.' This is the first and greatest commandment. And the second is like it: 'Love your neighbor as yourself.' All the Law and the Prophets hang on these two commandments."

- *Analysis of the decalogue reveals that it contains two parts: the first four commandments establish humanity's duties toward God (love of God) and the last six, humanity's duties toward their neighbor (love of neighbor). That's why Jesus summarizes this law in two great principles of love by declaring "on these two commandments hang all the law". This said, one cannot love God and neighbor while violating the precepts of this law.*

c. Its duration is eternal: Matt 5:17, 18; Luke 16:17

"Do not think that I have come to abolish the Law or the Prophets; I have not come to abolish them but to fulfill them." Matt 5:17

"It is easier for heaven and earth to disappear than for the least stroke of a pen to drop out of the Law." Luke 16:17

- *Some professing Christians often advance the opinion that Jesus's death on the cross abolished the law. Jesus's declaration is formal: "I have not come to abolish the Law or the Prophets". The moral law, by its character, cannot be abolished if it must regulate humans' relationships with each other and with their Creator.*

  Moreover, sin is the transgression of the law, that is, there is no sin without law. "For sin indeed was in the world before the law was given, but sin is not counted where there is no law." Rom 5:13(b). To claim that Jesus abolished the law is to implicitly say that He abolished sin; that is, He recommended theft, adultery, murder etc.

d. It is holy, just and perfect: Rom 7:12, 14; Ps 19:8

"So then, the law is holy, and the commandment is holy, righteous and good."

"The law of the Lord is perfect, refreshing the soul."

- *The moral law is perfect; this is not the case for other types of laws. For example:*

  1. *The ceremonial laws existed for a given circumstance, with a determined objective. They included types that prefigured Jesus and His sacrificial system. Circumstances having changed (that is, Jesus having died on the cross), there is necessarily a change of law; this is what the book of Hebrews indicates: "For when the priesthood is changed, the law must be changed also" Heb 7:12.*

2. *The laws relating to Israel's judicial system were only valid for a given circumstance: the theocracy where God also governs the people's temporal affairs. When Israel chose its political leaders and later became a nation like all others, these rules became inapplicable not only to Israel but also to any other people of the earth.*

However, it should be noted that certain moral principles contained in these laws cannot pass away because, by their essence, they are attached to the precepts of the mother-law (the decalogue) such as, for example: provisions relating to homosexuality, incest etc. (Lev 20:10-21).

e. It is the basis of judgment: James 2:8, 12; Rom 2:12

"Speak and act as those who are going to be judged by the law that gives freedom." James 2:12

"For it is not those who hear the law who are righteous in God's sight, but it is those who obey the law who will be declared righteous." Rom 2:13

- *The law is the criterion by which our life will be examined.*

f. It is one of the conditions established by Jesus for entering eternal life: Matt 19:16, 17

"And behold, a young man came and said to Him, 'Teacher, what good thing shall I do that I may have eternal life?' He said to him, 'Why do you ask Me about what is good? There is only One who is good. If you want to enter life, keep the commandments.'"

3. Can one omit a part of the law? James 2:9, 10

"For whoever keeps the whole law but fails in one point has become guilty of all of it." James 2:10

- *God's law must be observed in its entirety. No one can, at the risk of displeasing God, accept nine commandments and reject one.*

4. What was Jesus's attitude toward the law? 1 John 2:3-6, John 14:15

"**We** know that we have come to know him if we keep his commandments. Whoever says 'I know him' but does not keep his commandments is a liar, and the truth is not in him... Whoever says he abides in him ought to walk in the same way in which he walked."

- *Whoever says they know Jesus but does not keep His commandments is a liar, this is what the apostle John declares. And Jesus's commandments are not different from those of His Father. In His dialogue with the young man (Matt 19:18), He enumerated some of the commandments to show that He refers to the decalogue.*

5. What ultimate exhortation did Paul make concerning the commandments? 1 Cor 7:19

"**Circumcision** is nothing and uncircumcision is nothing. Keeping God's commands is what counts."

- *The decalogue, the only text of the Bible written directly by God's hands, represents a monument of extraordinary spiritual value. This law is moral because it presents moral principles defining human duties toward God (the first four commandments) and the six last ones, human duties toward neighbor. This is why Jesus summarizes them in two great commandments: Love God! Love your neighbor! It is curious to note that the decalogue has not been spared by human tradition: men often trying to correct God and even replace Him. Indeed, the second commandment of the sacred text dealing with the worship of images has been suppressed by men and to maintain the number of 10, the last commandment dealing with covetousness has been split in two.*

- *In summary, in concluding this study on God's law, it should be remembered that the law (Torah) mentioned at the beginning of this exposition is the expression of all God's instruction and teaching addressed to Israel, through Moses, in the Pentateuch. As such, it is not specific. It therefore includes and encompasses the different types of laws noted in the first five books of the Bible and highlighted in this study.*

RECAP: REFLECTION THEMES DRAWN FROM THIS STUDY:

1. List the different types of laws in the Bible
2. The two main parts of the decalogue
3. The Abolition of the law by Jesus
4. Can one omit a part of the law?
5. How should one who claims to know Jesus walk?

STUDY #11: UNDER THE LAW, UNDER GRACE

In a previous study, we saw Jesus affirm that He did not come to abolish the law. To a man who asked Him a question (Matt 19:16) about the conditions for having eternal life, He responds unambiguously: "If you want to enter life, keep the commandments". The Apostle James presents the law as needing to be observed in its entirety and as the basis for judgment (James 2:10, 12). But, in parallel, the Bible emphasizes another concept: grace, which is defined as unmerited favor, gift, source of salvation for all people. The big question is: "How to reconcile law and grace?" "Does one nullify or exclude the other?"

If we are saved by grace, why the law? How to resolve this dilemma or antinomy? Meanwhile, Paul declares "You are not under law, but under grace" (Rom 6:14). What does this affirmation of Paul imply and how to understand it? The Apostle Peter acknowledges that in Paul's writings "there are some things hard to understand, which untaught and unstable people twist to their own destruction" (2 Peter 3:16); this is why bringing clarity to the expression "Under the law, Under grace" is the objective of this study.

1. **How does the Bible define the source of salvation for all people? Ephesians 2:8**

"For it is by grace you have been saved, through faith—and this is not from yourselves, it is the gift of God."

- *We are saved by grace; and grace is an unmerited favor. This grace is manifested in that we were sinners condemned to die; Jesus came to die in our place, to give us eternal life. (John 3:16). It is by faith that we accept this salvation.*

2. **What are the roles of the law in salvation?**

   a. **Define and show sin: Rom 7:7, 8; Rom 5:13**

   "I would not have known what sin was had not the law said, 'You shall not covet.'" Rom 7:7(b) "For sin indeed was in the world before the law was given, but sin is not counted where there is no law." Rom 5:13

   - *The first role of the law is to define or show sin: there is no sin without law. And the wages of sin is death. The law cannot erase sin; it is only a mirror.*

   b. **Criterion or means of obedience: Rom 2:13**

   "For it is not those who hear the law who are righteous in God's sight, but it is those who obey the law who will be declared righteous"

   - *It is by observance of the law that we reveal our acceptance of this grace offered by Jesus on the cross. To have life, according to John 3:16, one must believe and this belief is not intellectual or virtual; it is real and translates into obedience.*

3. **What is the role of grace in salvation? Rom 5:17**

   "For if, by the trespass of the one man, death reigned through that one man, how much more will those who receive God's abundant provision of grace and of the gift of righteousness reign in life through the one man, Jesus Christ!"

   - *The role of grace is to erase and forgive sin to lead to eternal life. This is a fundamental difference between the role of law and that of grace: the law only shows sin; but it is grace that erases it through the blood of Jesus.*

4. **How to understand Paul's statement: "You are not under the law, but under grace" (Romans 6:14)**

- *What do the expressions "Being under the law" and "Being under grace" mean?*

- *Being under the law: It means disobeying a law and, as a result, being subject to the penalties attached to that law. In simple terms, it is being under the condemnation or judgment of the law.*

- *Being under grace: It means being released from the penalties attached to the violation of that law.*

- *• We were all sinners condemned to eternal death because the wages of sin is death. But Jesus, through His death, took our place, and we are now seen as innocent in the eyes of the Father. Should we therefore conclude that this grace or pardon has annulled the law that was violated? No! It would be absurd or senseless to say so, just as it would be foolish to claim that a driver who violated traffic laws and was pardoned without paying the penalties can now freely violate those laws without being guilty. Can it be said that the violated law is erased or annulled as a result of this grace? No!*

- *• As Paul said, we are no longer under the condemnation of the law because Jesus' death has removed that condemnation. From now on, we are candidates for eternal life. And because of this grace, as a sign of gratitude and love, we are more inclined to obey God's will.*

5. **What explanation does Paul give for his previous statement in Romans 6:14? (Romans 6:15)**

"What then? Shall we sin because we are not under the law but under grace? By no means!"

- *Here, in verse 15, Paul explains and clarifies verse 14. The phrase "Shall we sin" could also be translated as "Shall we transgress the law", since sin is the transgression of the law.*

6. **According to Paul, does faith annul the law? (Romans 3:31)**

"*Do we then nullify the law by this faith? Not at all! Rather, we uphold the law.*"

- *Instead of nullifying the law through faith, Paul says we confirm the law.*

7. How does James confirm that faith does not annul the law? (James 2:17-18, 20-26)

"In the same way, faith by itself, if it is not accompanied by action, is dead." (James 2:17) "As the body without the spirit is dead, so faith without deeds is dead." (James 2:26)

- *We must avoid seeing a contradiction or opposition between these statements of James and those of Paul. For example, Paul says: "Nevertheless, knowing that a person is not justified by the works of the law, but by faith in Jesus Christ." (Galatians 2:16)*

Both sets of statements explain the same reality: We are saved by grace, but by obeying God's law, we demonstrate our acceptance of this grace. In other words, we obey not to earn salvation but because we are saved. As members of God's kingdom, we naturally follow the rules that govern it. In simple terms, the works (obedience) we do are works of faith.

8. What other statements establish the necessity of obeying God? (1 John 5:3; Ecclesiastes 12:13)

"For this is the love of God: that we keep his commandments. And his commandments are not burdensome." (1 John 5:3) "Now all has been heard; here is the conclusion of the matter: Fear God and keep his commandments, for this is the duty of all mankind." (Ecclesiastes 12:15)

RECAP: KEY THEMES FOR REFLECTION FROM THIS STUDY

1. The role of the law in salvation.
2. The role of grace.
3. What does it mean to be "under the law"?
4. What does it mean to be "under grace"?

5. Does faith annul the law?

STUDY #12: THE DAY OF REST

Rest or pause is part of life's reality. One could never take the risk of running a vehicle or operating an engine twenty-four hours a day, for several weeks, without it being necessary to stop it at some point for technical maintenance. This would limit its lifespan or expose it to destruction altogether. The human body is like a machine; it needs rest, not only physical rest but also spiritual and mental rest. Man does not live by bread alone, says the Word of God; he also needs a moment in his life to recharge and reconnect with his Creator.

As God has always been concerned, since Eden, with humanity's complete fulfillment, this is undoubtedly what led Him, from the beginning, to provide a day of rest for humanity. Yes, the Bible speaks of a day of rest. But this important question has divided the Christian world into two major currents or groups: one worshiping God on Sunday and often doing so sincerely, with fervor; the other, making Saturday their day of worship and service. The astute observer wonders, perplexed, who to believe? or which of these practices conforms to biblical truth? Since we have learned, from the start, to make God's Word our only reference in doctrinal matters, we should consider, through this study, the Bible's teachings regarding the day of rest.

1. What did God do on the seventh day of creation? Gen 2:1-3

"Thus, the heavens and the earth were completed in all their vast array. By the seventh day God had finished the work he had been doing; so, on the seventh day, he rested from all his work. God blessed the seventh day and made it holy because on it he rested from all the work of creating that he had done."

- **Analysis of this passage reveals the following points:**

    1. **God rested**: God who created everything by a simple act of will, was not tired and, consequently, did not need rest. God's rest was for Him a moment to stop and contemplate the

creative work and, also and especially, a means of indicating to humanity, who would have to work and become tired, the necessity of resting.

2. **God rested on the seventh day**: but not just any day: the seventh

3. **Which day is the seventh of the week?** At creation, the days did not have names and were identified by an order number. The names of the days of the week later find their origin in the names of deities (stars and planets) of Roman mythology:

Sunday: Day of the Sun
Monday: Day of the Moon
Tuesday: Day of Mars
Wednesday: Day of Mercury
Thursday: Day of Jupiter
Friday: Day of Venus
Saturday: Day of Saturn

- To what order or number do these days of the week correspond? To answer this question, we need only remember that the Bible calls the "first day of the week" the day of Jesus's resurrection (Matt 28:1); this same day that universal history calls "Sunday". Thus, if Sunday is the first day of the week, Saturday is necessarily the seventh.

- Blessed and sanctified: By blessing the seventh day, the Creator made it a day different from the other six. In sanctifying it, He set it apart, that is, separated it for holy use.

It should be noted that this rest or sabbath was instituted by the Creator in Eden, at a time when the Jewish people were far from being constituted.

2. **For whom was the sabbath instituted? Mark 2:27; Isaiah 56:6, 7**

"Then he said to them, 'The Sabbath was made for man, not man for the Sabbath'" Mark 2:27

"And foreigners who bind themselves to the Lord to minister to him... who keep the Sabbath without desecrating it and who hold fast to my covenant... their burnt offerings and sacrifices will be accepted on my altar; for my house will be called a house of prayer for all nations" Isaiah 56:6, 7

- *The sabbath was made for man, that is, for all people, regardless of nationality, race, and origin. This said the sabbath was not made for the Jews. It was instituted at a time when there was not a Jew on earth. Man was created on the sixth day and the sabbath instituted on the seventh day, for man's happiness and fulfillment. The Sabbath, according to Isaiah 56, is also for "foreigners" who, in the bible, are identified as the Gentiles, the pagans, (non-Jews). These latter are included in God's plan of salvation, by adoption through the blood of Jesus. (Gal 3:29). The sabbath therefore belongs to all people.*

3. What is the fourth commandment of the Decalogue? Exodus 20:8-11

"**Reme**mber the Sabbath day by keeping it holy. Six days you shall labor and do all your work, but the seventh day is a sabbath to the Lord your God."

- *The "remember" well translates as a reminder of what has already been said. The Sabbath was not instituted at Mount Sinai at the time of the promulgation of the moral law, the Ten Commandments. This passage also recalls that: a) The Lord is the Creator b) The sabbath is the Lord's Day. In observing the sabbath, man does not make a gift or offering to the Lord; he only recognizes that this day belongs to Him.*

- *Through time, men have tried, in vain, to alter the seven-day weekly biblical rest cycle. During the French Revolution (from 1792 to 1806), the Republican or Revolutionary calendar sought to establish the décadi (from the Latin deca, meaning ten, and dies, meaning day), which was a rest cycle following every ten days of work. This change had significant consequences on economic and social activity, ultimately leading to a return to the weekly rest cycle prescribed by the Word of God.*

4. **For whom is the Sabbath a sign? Exodus 31:15-17; Ezekiel 20:12**

"**The Is**raelites are to observe the Sabbath... This will be a sign between me and the Israelites forever."

- *The sabbath is a distinctive sign of God's people, not only for Israel according to the flesh, but for those who constitute spiritual Israel or Israel by faith (Rom 2:29)*

5. **What description is given of the true sabbath observer? Isaiah 58:13, 14**

"**If you** keep your feet from breaking the Sabbath and from doing as you, please on my holy day... if you call the Sabbath a delight... if you honor it by not going your way and not doing as you, please or speaking idle words."

- *God calls the sabbath "my holy day"; which means that all our activities should be in harmony with the holiness of this day. This passage emphasizes that the sabbath is not only a cessation of physical and intellectual secular work but also a spiritual rest where one detaches from all ordinary activities to think about God.*

In exhorting us not to indulge "in our pleasures and idle talk", this passage forbids us, in the context of sanctifying this day:

- *Conversations on secular subjects*
- *Reading ordinary books and secular music*
- *Non-spiritual radio and television programs*

6. **Is there preparation to be made before the sabbath day? Mark 15:42; Exodus 16:4, 5, 23**

"**It was** Preparation Day (that is, the day before the Sabbath)" Mark 15:42

"On the sixth day, they are to prepare what they bring in, and that is to be twice as much as they gather on other days." Exodus 16:5

"This is what the Lord commanded: Tomorrow is to be a day of sabbath rest, a holy sabbath to the Lord. So, bake what you want to bake and boil what you want to boil. Save whatever is left and keep it until morning." Exodus 16:23

- *The day before the sabbath, the sixth day of the week (Friday) is called "the preparation". Very early in Israel's history, the Lord instructed this people about the importance of sabbath preparation. The day before, they were to gather a double portion of food, bake, and cook what was to be consumed on the sabbath day. This was a way of teaching Israel and every faithful sabbath observer that before sunset on the sixth day, everything must be ready: food, clothing, etc. to be able to commune, without hindrance, with God during His holy day.*

7. When does the sabbath begin and end? Gen 1:5, 8; Lev 23:27-28, 32

"**An**d there was evening, and there was morning—the first day... And there was evening, and there was morning—the second day."

- *According to the biblical definition, the day is the space between two evenings; therefore, sunset marks the beginning of the day which ends at the next sunset. This is why the sabbath begins at sunset on the sixth day (Friday) to ends the following day (Saturday). This said the opening and closing of the sabbath are not linked to a precise hour of the day.*

8. For how long will the sabbath be observed? Isaiah 66:22, 23

"'**As** the new heavens and the new earth that I make will endure before me,' declares the Lord, 'so will your name and descendants endure... From one New Moon to another and from one Sabbath to another, all mankind will come and bow down before me,' says the Lord."

- *Even on the new earth, the sabbath that will be observed represents an uninterrupted chain in man's relationships with God.*

9. **What relationship does the Bible establish between God's people and the sabbath? Heb 4:9, 10**

"There remains, then, a Sabbath rest for the people of God… for anyone who enters God's rest also rests from their works, just as God did from his."

- *From the passage above, formal logic allows us to conclude this: The sabbath rest is reserved for God's people, he or she who does not accept this rest says they are not part of God's people. The Sabbath is thus a sign of affiliation or belonging to God's people.*

Moreover, to avoid any misunderstanding or misinterpretation about the nature of this rest, the author of Hebrews specifies well: "Whoever enters this rest rests from their works, just as God rested from His", that is, a rest coming after six literal days as God rested from His labor.

- *The day of rest (sabbath) cited in Genesis 2 is indeed the seventh day of the week which corresponds to our Saturday in French. Originally, the days did not have names and were identified from their order number: 1st, 2nd, 3rd, etc… Over the ages, men gave them names in harmony with the worship given to certain stars (moon, sun) and certain planets, an approach which has in no way affected the order of days. The seventh day of the week, blessed by the Creator must be a source of happiness and benefit for man, sanctified (from Hebrew kahdash), means that it is consecrated, separated, and set apart for holy use.*

RECAP: REFLECTION THEMES DRAWN FROM THIS STUDY:

1. When and by whom was the Sabbath instituted?
2. For whom was the Sabbath instituted?
3. What is the republican calendar?
4. Which is the seventh day of the week?
5. When does the Sabbath begin and end?

STUDY #13: THE SABBATH IN CHRISTIANITY

The previous lesson taught us that the sabbath was instituted in Eden at a time when the Jewish people were not yet constituted; this said, the sabbath is not Jewish. This day of the week that the Lord calls "my holy day" is a day when man, detaching from earthly things, communes with his Creator, a way to thank Him for all that He is.

But the important questions to ask are: Is the sabbath still valid during the New Testament period? What was the behavior of Jesus and the Apostles concerning the Sabbath? Are there passages in the New Testament authorizing a change of worship from the seventh day to the first day of the week?

These pertinent questions call for answers that the present study proposes to provide.

1. Did Jesus observe His Father's commandments? John 15:10

"**If** you keep my commandments, you will remain in my love, just as I have kept my father's commandments and remain in his love."

- *It should be emphasized that Jesus's commandments were the same as those of His Father. In Matthew 22:36-40, Jesus presents two great commandments: Love God and Love your neighbor, which He says is the summary of all the law. Indeed, Jesus only confirmed the reality of the Decalogue whose first four commandments emphasize man's duties toward God, while the other six, his love for his neighbor. These are the commandments that Jesus invites His disciples to keep.*

2. What was Jesus's attitude toward the sabbath? Luke 4:16; Mark 2:28

"**He** went to Nazareth, where he had been brought up, and on the Sabbath day he went into the synagogue, as was his custom." Luke 4:16

"So, the Son of Man is Lord even of the Sabbath." Mark 2:28

- *Jesus had the custom of going to the synagogue on the sabbath day, as millions of people today have the custom of going to a place of worship, by the precepts of the fourth commandment: "Remember the Sabbath day by keeping it holy". Moreover, Jesus declares Himself to be the Master or Lord of the Sabbath, a way of saying that He would be the only one to have the authority to invalidate the validity of this day if it were needed.*

3. In what way should Jesus be our example? 1 John 2:6

"Whoever claims to live in him must live as Jesus did."

- *Being Christian or being a disciple of Jesus means walking in His footsteps: walking as He walked. The attitude of any Christian claiming to be a disciple of Jesus should be in no way different from that of Jesus toward the day of rest.*

4. How did Jesus make it understood that sabbath observance must be motivated by love? Luke 6:6-11

"**And** Jesus said to them, 'I ask you, is it lawful on the Sabbath to do good or to do harm, to save life or to destroy it?' Then he looked around at them all and said to the man, 'Stretch out your hand.' And he did so, and his hand was restored." Luke 6:9-10

- *The tradition of the Jews and Pharisees associated with sabbath observance a set of human prescriptions that made it a burden. For example, the question of whether one could heal a sick person on the sabbath day. Jesus's attitude, through these passages, is a way of stripping sabbath observance of the dross they had introduced into it and showing future generations that observance of the commandments, in general, and of the sabbath, in particular, must be an expression of love. This said any physical or material activities tending to relieve or heal a sick or endangered person are in no way a violation of the Sabbath. On the contrary, all this is quite consistent with the spirit of the sabbath, as taught by Jesus.*

5. **What relationship does the New Testament establish between Jesus's resurrection and the sabbath? Matt 28:1; Mark 16:1, 2**

"**After t**he Sabbath, at dawn on the first day of the week, Mary Magdalene and the other Mary went to look at the tomb." Matt 28:1

- *The expression "After the Sabbath, at dawn on the first day of the week" clearly establishes that the first day of the week or Sunday comes after the sabbath or rest; this said, the first day of the week is not the sabbath or rest.*

6. **On what day did the women who followed Jesus rest? Luke 23:55, 56**

"**The w**omen who had come with Jesus from Galilee followed Joseph and saw the tomb and how his body was laid in it. Then they went home and prepared spices and perfumes. But they rested on the Sabbath in obedience to the commandment."

- *These women who constantly accompanied Jesus knew well the importance that the Savior gave to the sabbath; even at His death, they did not dare violate it and thus proved that Jesus's death on the cross does not nullify the sabbath. If it were otherwise, they would be the first to know it and apply it.*

7. **Did the early Churches and Apostles observe the Sabbath?**

a. **Church of Antioch: Acts 13:13-14, 42-44**

"From Paphos, Paul and his companions sailed to Perga... On the Sabbath, they went into the synagogue and sat down. When they came out, they invited them to speak further about these matters on the next Sabbath... On the next Sabbath almost, the whole city gathered to hear the word of the Lord."

b. **Church of Philippi: Acts 16:12, 13**

"From there we went to Philippi, a Roman colony and the leading city of that district of Macedonia... On the Sabbath, we went outside the city gate to the river, where we expected to find a place of prayer. We sat down and began to speak to the women who had gathered there."

- *Here, Paul spends a sabbath in nature, by the sea, with the Christians of the Church of Philippi.*

c. *Church of Thessalonica: Acts 17:1, 2*

"Paul and Silas traveled through Amphipolis and Apollonia and came to Thessalonica, where there was a Jewish synagogue... As was his custom, Paul went into the synagogue, and on three Sabbath days he reasoned with them from the Scriptures."

- *This passage reveals that the Apostle had the custom of going to the synagogue on the sabbath day, as millions of Christians throughout the world still do today. He spends three sabbaths with the Christians of Thessalonica to discuss with them according to the Scriptures.*

d. *Church of Corinth: Acts 18:1, 4, 11*

"After this, Paul left Athens and went to Corinth... Every Sabbath he reasoned in the synagogue, trying to persuade Jews and Greeks... So, Paul stayed in Corinth for a year and a half, teaching them the word of God."

- *Paul spends about seventy-eight (78) sabbaths teaching God's word to the Church of Corinth.*

8. How does Jesus indicate that the sabbath should be observed after His death? Matt 24:20

"**P**ray that your flight will not take place in winter or on the Sabbath." Matt 24:20

- *This declaration by Jesus confirms that He recognizes that the sabbath would exist long after His death, which occurred around the year 31 CE. Indeed, in the year 70 CE, about forty years after Jesus's death, the Roman army led by Titus besieged and destroyed the city and temple of Jerusalem. Thus, as many other biblical passages prove, the sabbath remains in force after Jesus's death, as it will be until the new earth.*

9. **Is there a passage in the New Testament indicating a change of sanctification from the seventh day to the first day of the week? Matt 28:1; John 20:1, 19; Luke 24:1; Mark 16:2, 9; Acts 20:7; 1 Cor 16:2**

- *The expression the first day of the week is mentioned eight (8) times in the New Testament (see the passages indicated above). Six of these texts refer to Jesus's resurrection, and none of them makes any allusion to a transfer of worship from the seventh to the first day of the week. If it were to be so, it is really in these texts that this should be indicated. In summary, the rest of the seventh day of the week, instituted by God in Eden and observed by Jesus and the apostles, remains in force during Christianity and will be observed until the new earth.*

RECAP: REFLECTION THEMES DRAWN FROM THIS STUDY:

1. Did Jesus observe the Sabbath?
2. Did the apostles observe the Sabbath?
3. Can one cite a text from the New Testament indicating a change in rest?
4. Contrary to the Pharisees, what meaning did Jesus give to the Sabbath
5. Did Jesus observe His Father's commandments?

STUDY #14: ORIGIN OF SUNDAY OBSERVANCE

We have said in one of the studies that the Christian world is divided into two major groups: one making the first day of the week or Sunday their day of worship; the other, the seventh day of the week or Saturday. If, through these two studies, it has been shown, using God's Word, the origin of the sabbath, the seventh day of the week, the big question to ask is: "What is the origin of Sunday observance as a day of rest?" The most common answer is: "We chose Sunday to honor and commemorate the day of Jesus's resurrection". Two (2) points should be emphasized in this answer: 1- "We chose" 2- "The day of Jesus's resurrection"

The first element namely "we chose" denotes a certain sincerity; that is, we recognize that it is "we who chose". This raises a question: "Can we choose in place of God or give Him what we want?" The second element is: the "Day of Jesus's resurrection". This point raises,, two (2) questions, despite the importance of this event: 1- Does the Bible indicate that the day of the resurrection should replace the rest of the seventh day? 2- Since when was an anniversary celebrated every week, instead of being an annual feast?

These questions and others will find their answer in the exposition that follows.

1. **What did Paul announce about the apostasy that should happen to the Christian Church? Acts 20:29, 30**

"I know that after I leave, savage wolves will come in among you and will not spare the flock. Even from your own number men will arise and distort the truth in order to draw away disciples after them."

- *Paul had well announced, by this declaration, that men would come to teach pernicious things, that is, teachings that have no scriptural basis. Through time, history is full of examples where men have tried to correct God and even replace Him with their traditions.*

2. **When Israel turned away from God, what did they do? 2 Kings 23:5; Ezekiel 6:4**

"**He did** away with the idolatrous priests appointed by the kings of Judah to burn incense on the high places of the towns of Judah and those around Jerusalem—those who burned incense to Baal, to the sun and moon, to the constellations and all the starry hosts." 2 Kings 23:5

- *God's people, throughout their history, have known moments of apostasy. When they turned away from the Lord, they went to worship the moon, the sun, and the host of heaven. The worship of the sun is not only a dominant point in the life of pagan peoples but also of apostate Israel.*

3. **When men turned to sun worship, what did they do with the Lord's Sabbath? Ezekiel 20:24**

"**Because** they had not obeyed my laws but had rejected my decrees and desecrated my Sabbaths, and their eyes lusted after their parents' idols."

- *They despised the Lord's sabbath when they turned to the worship of idols, that is, of created things.*

4. **Which day was dedicated to sun worship?**

- *The first day of the week (Sunday) was dedicated to the sun and its worship throughout pagan antiquity. In English, "Sunday" or Dimanche (day of the sun); in German, "Sontag" or Dimanche (day of the sun).*

5. **How did the transition from the day of the sun (Sunday) to the Christian day of rest occur?**

- *On **March 7, 321** CE, Constantine, the first Roman Emperor converted to Christianity, decreed Sunday (the first day of the week) as the weekly day of rest. He thus wanted to bring pagans closer to Christians through the day of rest. This day becomes for Christians the "dies Dominicus", the Lord's Day, the origin of the French word "Dimanche".*

- *"The reason why we observe the first day of the week instead of the seventh rests on no positive command. It is in vain that one would search the Scriptures for a justification of a substitution of the first for the seventh day. The first Christians began to worship God on the first day of the week because Jesus was resurrected from the dead on this day. Then, little by little, this day of worship also became a day of worship, a legal holiday in the year 321. This is why our Christian sabbath does not rely on a positive command, it is a gift from the Church." (C G. Chappel, Methodist author, Ten rules for living, Abingdon-Cokensbury Press, New York-Nashville, 1938, p. 61)*

- *"The observation of Sunday succeeded under the new law to the observation of the Sabbath, not by the precept, but according to the institution of the Church and the custom of the Christian people."*

(Thomas Aquinas, Theological Sum, question CXXII, article V, 4, trans. By Abbé Drioux, Paris, 1852, t.V, p. 184)

6. Was this prophecy relating to this change announced? Dan 7:25

"He shall speak words against the Highest, and shall wear out the saints of the Highest, and shall think to change the times and the law."

- *This prophecy of Daniel, to be well understood, must be placed in the context of the vision of the four beasts (Dan 7:1-28). Indeed, these four beasts represent four universal empires that should emerge from the earth (v.17): Babylon, Medes/Persia, Greece, Rome. Just as the fourth beast had ten horns, from which came a little horn different from the others, Rome, the fourth world empire was broken up and, on its ruins, emerge ten first states of Europe, after the barbarian powers divided the spoils of this kingdom. Thus, just as the ten horns, the little horn came out of Rome, the fourth empire. The only power which, in history, corresponds to the description given by Daniel, relating to this little horn, is the Papacy or religious Rome.*

- *The prophecy indicates that this power should take the initiative to change the times and the law, as attested by the following excerpts:*

  1. **"The pope holds such great authority and power that he can modify, explain or interpret even divine laws." Papa II, p. 18**

  2. In the catechisms, God's law has been changed and virtually promulgated by the papacy: **"The second commandment which forbids the making and worship of images is omitted, and the tenth which forbids coveting is divided into two."** (Review & Herald Pub. Assoc., 1942) p. 221

  3. **"The Church's authority is highlighted to the highest degree by the Scriptures since it recommends them, declares them divine, and delivers them for our reading. The Sabbath day of the law that we celebrate is transferred to the Lord's Day. This precept, as well as other similar articles, did not end by Christ's teaching (he** said he came to fulfill the law and not to abolish it), but have been changed

by the authority of the Church" ***Sacrorum Conciliorum Nova et amplississima Collectio, Paris-Leipzig, 1902***

7. Has the Roman Church claimed responsibility for these changes?

To answer this question, see the following excerpts as reference:

a) (Ref: Catechism of Catholic doctrine, Rev. Pierre Guermann 3rd edition 1913, page 50)

Question: *Which is the Sabbath day?*

Answer: *Saturday is the Sabbath day*

Question: *Why do we observe Sunday instead of Saturday?*

Answer: *We observe Sunday instead of Saturday because the Catholic Church at its Council of Laodicea transferred the solemnity from Saturday to Sunday.*

b) (Catechism of Trent, 1566, page 347 by S. Donovan)

"It has pleased the Church to transfer the celebration of the Sabbath day to the Lord's Day; for on this day the sun first shone on the world, thus by the resurrection of our Redeemer on this day, he has opened for us the door to eternal life, our life has been recalled from darkness to light"

8. Whom should we obey? Acts 5:29

"Peter and the other apostles replied: 'We must obey God rather than human beings!'"

- *The call that is launched to humanity is clear: obey God rather than men. In summary, to answer the question: What is the origin of Sunday as a day of rest? we must not seek this answer in the Bible (New and Old Testament), we must go especially to pagan antiquity and human tradition.*

- *While recognizing that the Reformation of the 16th century, which saw the birth of Protestantism, is the greatest religious movement of all time, it must also be admitted that the slogan "Sola Scriptura" (Scripture alone) advocated by this movement has been misused and betrayed. Sunday observance as a day of rest is an inheritance from the Roman Church transmitted to Protestantism, without the latter being able to justify it biblically. It is rightly said that Protestantism is the legitimate daughter of the Roman Church.*

RECAP: REFLECTION THEMES DRAWN FROM THIS STUDY

1. Day of resurrection (Sunday) and day of rest.

2. Day of worship in pagan antiquity.

3. Indicate the year of Constantine's decree establishing the 1st day as rest.

4. Has the Roman Church claimed these changes? Which ones?

5. Recall at least two changes made to the decalogue.

STUDY #15: WHY BE BAPTIZED?

In general, when two people decide to start a joint venture, they sign a document or contract in front of a state representative that establishes the rights and responsibilities of both parties. The same is true for marriage. When two people love each other and want to unite for life, they must appear before a religious minister or public official to sign a contract where both solemnly declare they want to take each other as husband and wife. The same reality exists in the spiritual realm. When a person receives the Gospel message, is penetrated by its truth, and wants to follow Jesus, they enter their heart into a relationship of love with the Savior. But this intimate and personal decision must be consecrated by a public and solemn act: Baptism.

While it is true that baptism is at the heart of all Christian religions, it is also true that there are different meanings and contents attached to this site. Why? Why speak sometimes of baptism by sprinkling or pouring, sometimes of baptism by immersion? What is the meaning and importance of baptism considering God's Word?

1. **What fundamental condition did Jesus establish for entering God's kingdom? John 3:3,5**

"Jesus answered and said to him, 'Most assuredly, I say to you, unless one is born again, he cannot see the kingdom of God...Most assuredly, I say to you, unless one is born of water and the Spirit, he cannot enter the kingdom of God.'"

- *During Jesus' encounter with Nicodemus, a Jewish leader, His declaration is formal: To enter God's kingdom, one must be born again and this new birth implies two corollaries: a) Born of water, referring to the baptism of the body. b) Born of Spirit, referring to change of heart and mind. In short, the new birth implies a radical change, a total transformation of one is being, and a new direction for their life.*

2. **What instruction did Jesus give to His disciples? Matt 28:19,20; Mark 16:16**

"Go therefore and make disciples of all nations, baptizing them in the name of the Father and of the Son and the Holy Spirit" Matt 28:19

"He who believes and is baptized will be saved, but he who does not believe will be condemned" Mark 16:16

- *Matt 28:19 presents a solemn injunction made to all who believe. Those who have heard God's voice speaking to them and who feel the intimate need to follow Him and draw near to Him must be baptized. Baptism is therefore an external act, a public demonstration, an unequivocal testimony that one has received Jesus in their heart and is determined to walk with Him throughout life.*

3. **What is the significance of baptism? Rom 6:3,4**

"Or do you not know that as many of us as were baptized into Christ Jesus were baptized into His death? Therefore, we were buried with Him through baptism into death, that just as Christ was raised from the dead by the glory of the Father, even so we also should walk in newness of life"

- *This passage reveals that the rite of baptism involves two symbolic gestures: 1- The death of the old man and his burial in Jesus' death. 2- The resurrection of a new man, in the image of Christ's resurrection, to lead a new life.*

The only form of baptism recognized by the Bible and practiced by Jesus and the Apostles is baptism by immersion. The word baptism comes from the Greek "baptizo" which means: to plunge, to immerse. There can be no baptism without immersion, for it commemorates the death and resurrection of our Lord. Water baptism thus symbolizes the death of the old man, the burial of the past, and resurrection to lead a new life in Christ. Baptism by sprinkling introduced by human tradition into Christianity is a breach of both the spirit and letter of the sacred book.

4. How did Jesus give His disciples the example of the form of baptism? Matt 3:13,16

"Then Jesus came from Galilee to John at the Jordan to be baptized by him... When He had been baptized, Jesus came up immediately from the water"

- *To administer baptism requires much water. The expression "came up from the water" means that Jesus had gone down into the water, to be immersed, thus consecrating the symbolism of baptism by immersion.*

5. How does Paul confirm the existence of only one form of baptism? Eph 4:5

"One Lord, one faith, one baptism"

- *Paul confirms that there exists only one form or type of baptism: by immersion*

6. *What* experiences must precede baptism? Mark 16:16; Acts 2:38,41 "He who believes and is baptized will be saved" Mark 16:16(a)

"Then Peter said to them, 'Repent, and let every one of you be baptized in the name of Jesus Christ... Then those who gladly received his word were baptized'" Acts 2:38,41

- *Belief and repentance must precede the decision to be baptized. Evangelical baptism is a commitment that can only be made by a lucid person, conscious of their state. Belief precedes baptism; a baby of a few months cannot, consequently, be baptized, about the prescripts of the inspired Word. This commitment is personal, meaning it cannot be made by proxy: by a father, mother, or third party.*

7. Can One Be Saved by Proxy? Ezekiel 14:19-20

"Or if I send a plague into that land and pour out my wrath on it through bloodshed, killing its people and their animals, as surely as I live, declares the Sovereign Lord, even if Noah, Daniel, and Job were in it, they could save neither son nor daughter. They would save only themselves by their righteousness."

- This passage underscores a vital spiritual principle: salvation cannot be obtained by proxy. Everyone is accountable for their faith and righteousness before God. Even the exemplary lives of great figures like Noah, Daniel, and Job cannot save others—only their faith and righteousness could deliver them.

- This teaching emphasizes the personal responsibility of each believer to seek and maintain their relationship with God. While intercessory prayer and guidance from others are valuable, salvation is ultimately an individual journey of faith, repentance, and obedience.

Salvation is personal and individual. Children cannot be saved because of their parents' obedience, and parents cannot take any commitment before God on behalf of their children.

8. What Did the Ethiopian Eunuch Ask After Hearing Philip's Preaching? Acts 8:35-38

"Then Philip opened his mouth, and beginning at this Scripture, preached Jesus to him. Now as they went down the road, they came to some water. And the eunuch said, 'See, here is water. What hinders me from being baptized?' So, he commanded the chariot to stand still. And both Philip and the eunuch went down into the water, and he baptized him." (Acts 8:35-38)

- Those who believe must be baptized. The natural reaction of every believer is to request baptism. This passage emphasizes immersion (*"they both went down into the water"*).

9. What Should Be the Experience of a Baptized Believer? Coloss 3: 1,2

"If then you were raised with Christ, seek those things which are above, where Christ is, sitting at the right hand of God. Set your mind on things above, not on things on the earth." (Colossians 3:1-2)

- A baptized believer is called to live a new life in Christ. Paul further confirms this when he declares: *"For you were once darkness, but now you are light in the Lord. Walk as children of light."* (Ephesians 5:8)

10. Can One Be Baptized More Than Once? Acts 19:1-5

"Did you receive the Holy Spirit when you believed?" they answered, "No, we have not even heard that there is a Holy Spirit." So, Paul asked, "Then what baptism did you receive?" "John's baptism," they replied. On hearing this, they were baptized in the name of the Lord Jesus." (Acts 19:1-5)

Baptism should be the result or expression of faith. The passage indicates that these disciples had previously been baptized under John's baptism. However, upon learning of the Holy Spirit and believing in Christ, they were baptized again in the name of the Lord Jesus. This shows that rebaptism is appropriate when there is a new understanding or belief that deepens one's faith in Christ. But, without being fully instructed in the truth—specifically, the knowledge of the Holy Spirit. They were baptized a second time to express their acceptance of this new belief. While they were baptized a second time, it was still the same and singular baptism: baptism by immersion.

11. Who Should Be Baptized?

There are approximately three categories of people:

1. Those who have never received evangelical baptism.

- This includes individuals who were baptized as infants or children through sprinkling or pouring, practices not aligned with biblical teachings.

2. Those who were baptized once, by immersion, but were not fully instructed in all truth at the time of their decision.

- As in Acts 19, a new baptism signifies their solemn acceptance and faith in new convictions.

3. Those who were previously baptized by immersion but have renounced their Christian calling

- Displaying a lifestyle contrary to Christian ideals, they have been severed from the Body of Christ (the Church). A renewed decision and baptism are required to reintegrate them.

12. Can One Reject God's Call Without Consequence? John 12:47-48:

"If anyone hears my words but does not keep them, I do not judge that person. For I did not come to judge the world, but to save the world. There is a judge for the one who rejects me and does not accept my words; the very words I have spoken will condemn them at the last day."

Luke 14:16-20: The parable of the great banquet highlights those who reject God's invitation by offering excuses, ultimately facing exclusion from the feast prepared by the Lord.

- Rejection of God's call is not without consequence. The very Word of God, offered for salvation, becomes the basis for judgment if it is rejected.

RECAP: Reflection Themes drawn from This Study

1. What are the two symbolic movements of baptism?
2. Where and how was Jesus baptized?
3. What Experiences Should Precede Baptism?
4. How Many Forms of Baptism Does the Bible Recognize?

STUDY #16: THE STATE OF THE DEAD AND SPIRITISM

From ancient times, the question of death has haunted humanity. People have long sought to lift the veil separating them from the departed, asking: "What is the state of a person at death?" This question has been addressed differently across civilizations and religious beliefs.

A second question naturally arises: "Can the dead and the living communicate?" This query gave rise to a doctrine known as spiritism, which claims to provide answers. However, given the debates and contradictions surrounding this topic, it is essential to turn to Scripture for clarity:

1. **What Does the Bible Say About the State of a Person at Death? Ecclesiastes 9:4-6, 10**

   "Anyone who is among the living has hope—even a live dog is better off than a dead lion! For the living know that they will die, but the dead know nothing; they have no further reward, and even their name is forgotten. Their love, their hate, and their jealousy have long since vanished; never again will they have a part in anything that happens under the sun."

   Psalm 146:3-4 "Do not put your trust in princes, in human beings, who cannot save. When their spirit departs, they return to the ground; on that very day their plans come to nothing."

   - These passages establish the unconscious state of the dead. The dead have no awareness, memory, or involvement in earthly matters.

   Implications for Spiritism and Practices Involving the Dead: Any practice aimed at contacting the dead has no scriptural basis.

   - Worshiping the dead or invoking them is rooted in the theory of the immortality of the soul, which contradicts biblical teachings.

   These passages demonstrate that the dead have no awareness, consciousness, or involvement in earthly matters. Consequently, any practice aimed at contacting the dead is without scriptural basis. The worship of the dead is rooted in the theory of the immortality of the soul or the continued existence of the deceased. This necessitates an analysis of the various meanings of the concept of the *soul* (*"âme"*) as presented in the Bible

2. What Are the Different Meanings of "Soul" in the Bible?

a. Soul as a Living Person: Genesis 2:7

"The Lord God formed man from the dust of the ground and breathed into his nostrils the breath of life, and the man became a living soul."

1 Corinthians 15:45: *"So it is written: 'The first man Adam became a living soul'; the last Adam, a life-giving spirit."*

These passages show that the soul is not a separate entity placed by God into a human body. Instead, the human became a living soul when the breath of life was introduced into the lifeless form of Adam. The soul is thus the living person—a result of life within the physical body. It is not an independent, separable entity.

This understanding confirms that the soul is mortal: "The soul who sins shall die." (Ezekiel 18:4)

b. Soul as Blood: Leviticus 17:14:

"For the life of every creature is its blood: its blood is its life."

In biblical language, *soul* and *blood* are often used interchangeably to signify physical life. The life (*soul*) is considered to reside in the blood and ceases at death.

A. Antomarchi notes: *"It is repeatedly stated in Leviticus and elsewhere that physical life and soul are interchangeable terms, and that life, like the soul, is in the blood; both are extinguished at death."* (**Aux écoutes de l'Esprit**, Privas, 1952, p. 47)

c. Soul as the Seat of Emotions and Feelings

In a philosophical sense, the *soul* may also refer to an aspect of the individual encompassing emotions and sentiments. For example, a person's *soul* can experience joy or sorrow depending on their emotional state.

Mark 13:34: *"He said to them, 'My soul is overwhelmed with sorrow to the point of death. Stay here and keep watch.*

"Now my soul is troubled. And what shall I say? Father, save me from this hour." — *John 12:27 "And my soul shall be joyful in the Lord; it shall rejoice in His salvation."* — *Psalm 35:9*

Even in relation to these considerations, where the soul refers to emotions and feelings, one cannot speak of the immortality of the soul, because the emotions and feelings of a person cannot exist outside that person.

- *Worship of the Dead and the Immortality of the Soul*

The worship of the dead, which originates from ancient paganism, is widely practiced today. On the one hand, it is observed by followers of occult sciences (like voodoo), and on the other hand, by a significant portion of Catholic Christians. A specific date each year (November 1st) is officially dedicated as "All Saints' Day".

On this occasion, millions of people, with rare piety, fill cemeteries to place a wreath of flowers on the grave of a deceased relative or to offer a prayer there. These practices are strongly influenced by the belief that the dead can communicate their will to the living through dreams or other particular signs.

The faithful are encouraged to pray constantly for their deceased relatives or friends. In terms of historical development, the year 190 AD marks the beginning of prayers for the dead. Later, in 1439 AD, the doctrine of purgatory was officially recognized. The term "purgatory" comes from the Latin "purgare", meaning "to purge." According to this doctrine, which is not recognized by the Bible, deceased persons who have not committed so-called "mortal sins" serve a transitional period of punishment before being transferred to eternal bliss.

3. *What is Spiritism?*

Spiritism, which is based on the belief in the immortality of the soul, is the doctrine that at death, an immaterial part called the "soul or spirit" separates from the body. This spirit is said to have the ability to manifest and make contact with the living through intermediaries known as "mediums."

4. *What Does the Bible Say About the Worship of the Dead and Spiritism?*

Leviticus 19:31 — *"Do not turn to those who evoke spirits or to fortune tellers; do not seek them out, so that you will not be defiled by them. I am the Lord your God."*

Leviticus 20:6 — *"If anyone turns to the dead and the spirits to prostitute himself with them, I will set my face against that person and will cut him off from his people."*

Leviticus 20:27 — *"If a man or a woman has in them a spirit of the dead or a spirit of divination, they shall be put to death; they shall be stoned; their blood shall be upon them."*

Deuteronomy 18:9-12 — *"When you enter the land that the Lord your God is giving you, do not learn to imitate the detestable ways of the nations there. Let no one be found among you who sacrifices their son or daughter in the fire, who practices divination or sorcery, interprets omens, engages in witchcraft, casts spells, or who is a medium or spiritist or who consults the dead. Anyone who does these things is detestable to the Lord, and because of these detestable practices, the Lord your God will drive out those nations before you."*

Based on these formal statements of the Holy Scriptures, according to which the dead cannot engage in any activity before the resurrection (Ecclesiastes 9:6), those who claim to communicate with the dead are, in reality, interacting with occult or satanic powers.

5. *Can Satan Do Extraordinary Things?*

Matthew 24:24 — *"For false messiahs and false prophets will appear and perform great signs and wonders to deceive, if possible, even the elect."*

2 Corinthians 11:14 — *"And no wonder, for Satan himself masquerades as an angel of light."*

"The doctrine of the conscious state of the dead, and especially the belief in the return of the spirits of the dead to minister to the living, is essentially pagan and has paved the way for modern spiritualism. The fallen angels, under the control of Satan, appear in these spiritist ceremonies as messengers from the spirit world... Satan has the power to present before men the appearance of their deceased friends. The counterfeit is perfect; the familiar features, the words, and the tone of voice are reproduced with amazing clarity. Many are comforted by the assurance that their loved ones are enjoying heavenly bliss, and, unsuspecting of danger, they lend an ear to seducing spirits and doctrines of demons." Ellen G. White, The Great Controversy, pp. 485-486:

"For my part, I believe, and I know the truth and reality of many of the so-called spiritist phenomena. I can only affirm with greater force my experimental conviction that these phenomena are, or may be, of diabolical origin and, in any case, favor the work of the devil." Valentin Bresie, Director of Thesaurus Sapientae, Encyclopedia of Poetry, Esotericism, and Symbolism (Thesaurus Sapientae, Mercure Universel, Non-commercial Edition, Paris, 1948, 1079 p.16):

6. **What Is the Bible's Ultimate Exhortation Concerning Spiritism?**

Isaiah 8:19 — *"When someone tells you to consult mediums and spiritists, who whisper and mutter, should not a people inquire of their God? Why consult the dead-on behalf of the living?"*

RECAP OF KEY POINTS FROM THIS STUDY

1. *According to the Bible, are the dead conscious?*
2. *List three (3) meanings of the concept of the "soul."*
3. *What is Spiritism?*
4. *Cite Bible verses that condemn the worship of the dead and spiritism.*
5. *Recall the following key dates:*
- *The beginning of prayers for the dead*

- *The official recognition of the doctrine of purgatory*

STUDY #17: THE BIBLE AND MY HEALTH

Health is the most precious asset of humanity. History is full of examples of wealthy but sick people who offered their fortunes in exchange for health and life, but without success. It has been wrongly believed that God is only concerned with our future eternal life, without caring much about our physical life here on Earth — that is, our health and our bodies. Many think that their body belongs to them and that they can do with it as they please, in one way or another, and that God has nothing to do with it.

However, it seems that the matter is quite different when, under the inspiration of the Holy Spirit, the Apostle John says to Gaius: "Beloved, I wish above all things that you may prosper and be in health, even as your soul prospers." — 3 John 2

Yes! God wants us to prosper, not only spiritually but also physically. In short, God wants us to be in good health.

1. **What warning is given regarding how we should manage our bodies?1 Corinthians 6:19-20; 1 Corinthians 3:17**

   "Do you not know that your body is the temple of the Holy Spirit who is in you, whom you have received from God? You are not your own... Glorify God in your body and in your spirit, which belong to God." — 1 Corinthians 6:19-20

   "If anyone destroys the temple of God, God will destroy him; for the temple of God is holy, and that is what you are." — *1 Corinthians 3:17*

These passages remind us that:

1. We do not belong to ourselves; our body belongs to God, for He is our Creator.

2. Our body, as the temple of God, is holy.

3. If anyone destroys this temple, God will destroy him. This means that we do not have the right to treat our bodies as we please; we are accountable to God.

2. How can one destroy their body?

a) *By how we treat it*

The pursuit of money and material goods often causes us to work excessively, without rest. In this way, we are unknowingly destroying our health.

b) *By introducing harmful substances into it*

Although the Bible is not a health manual, it teaches us to avoid anything that destroys the "temple of God" — our body — or anything that diminishes our mental and physical faculties.

1. *Tobacco*

"Tobacco use is the leading preventable cause of death worldwide. Its consumption often leads to heart and lung diseases. Smoking significantly increases the risk of heart attacks, strokes, chronic obstructive pulmonary disease (COPD), emphysema, and cancer, especially lung cancer." — (Wikipedia)

"Filtered cigarettes and cigarettes low in nicotine and tar do not provide any guarantee to smokers against respiratory diseases. In fact, certain respiratory toxins are more concentrated in them and even pass through the filter: these include (a) carbon monoxide, which increases the risk of heart attack, (b) hydrogen cyanide (HCN), (c) aldehydes, and (d) acrolein, a highly toxic substance used as a chemical weapon during the First World War." (Alerte, 1980)

2. **Alcohol**

"Alcohol can cause numerous diseases, including cancers (mouth, esophagus, throat), liver diseases (cirrhosis), pancreatic diseases, nervous system disorders, and psychological issues (anxiety, depression, irritability, etc.)." — Dr. Jesus Cardenas (March 2018)

3. What does the Word of God say about strong drinks? Isaiah 5:11, 22; Proverbs 23:31-33

"Woe to those who rise early in the morning to run after strong drink, and who linger late at night as wine inflames them... Woe to those who are champions at drinking wine and heroes at mixing strong drink." — *Isaiah 5:11, 22*

- *"Through these passages, the Bible warns those who are bold enough to chase after intoxicating drinks or mix strong liquors. By 'strong liquors,' one should understand 'alcoholic beverages.'*

- *It is worth noting that 'some authors differentiate between the terms "alcoholized" (when alcohol is added) and "alcoholic" (when alcohol is present without being added, as in the case of fermentation). This distinction is not universally established, as the terms "alcoholized" and "alcoholic" can both mean "containing alcohol"'** (Free Encyclopedia - Wikipedia).*

- *Furthermore, it is important to highlight two (2) statements made by the apostle Paul on this subject:*

- *"Do not get drunk with wine, for that is debauchery" (Ephesians 5:18)*

- *"Stop drinking only water, and use a little wine because of your stomach and your frequent illnesses" (1 Timothy 5:23)*

- *By comparing these passages with other biblical verses such as Isaiah 5:11-12, some Christians conclude that the restriction on the consumption of alcoholic beverages is relative. It takes into account, on the one hand, the alcohol content of the beverage and, on the other hand, the frequency with which these drinks are consumed. Such reasoning naturally leads certain professing Christians to believe that they are allowed, on rare and exceptional occasions, to consume a small amount of low-alcohol beverages without feeling guilty. However, these practices naturally contrast with another current that advocates total and complete abstinence from alcohol, such as the position held by the Seventh-day Adventist Church."*

4. **According to medical advice, what are two key factors for good health?**

1. *Physical exercise, sport*

People who engage in regular physical activities tend to be healthier. Activities like walking, running, or jogging help eliminate body fat and improve brain function, while reducing the risk of chronic diseases.

2. *Healthy diet*

A healthy diet is one that is balanced and varied, prioritizing fresh foods over processed ones. It also involves limiting the intake of sugar, salt, and fats. This reflects the principle of "eating less, but eating better."

5. **What diet was given to humans at creation? Genesis 1:29**

"Then God said, 'Behold, I have given you every herb bearing seed, which is upon the face of all the earth, and every tree that has fruit with seed in it; they will be yours for food.'

It is clear that the original diet given by God at creation was vegetarian.

6. **When did God permit humans to eat meat? Genesis 9:1-4**
"Every moving thing that lives shall be food for you; as I gave you the green plants, I now give you everything. But you shall not eat flesh with its life, that is, its blood."

After the flood, when the vegetation had been destroyed, God permitted humans to consume meat.

7. *Does God make a distinction between animals? Genesis 7:2*

"Take with you seven pairs of every clean animal, a male and its mate, and a pair of the animals that are not clean, a male and its mate."

From the beginning, God distinguished between clean and unclean animals, and only God, as the Creator, knows the reasons for this classification.

8. ***What restrictions were made on the consumption of meat?*** *Leviticus 11:1-47*

   a. **Animals in general: v. 3, 4**

   "You may eat any animal that has a split hoof, completely divided, and that chews the cud... But you must not eat those that only chew the cud or only have a split hoof."

   b. **Animals in the waters (seas, rivers): v. 9, 10**

   "Of all the creatures living in the water, you may eat any that have fins and scales, whether in the seas or in the rivers."

   c. **Birds and their species: v. 13-19**

   "These are the birds you are to regard as detestable and must not eat."

   d. **Four-legged animals that walk on their paws: v. 27**

   "Of all the animals that walk on all fours, those that walk on their paws you are to regard as unclean."

9. **What does the Bible say about pork?** *Leviticus 11:7*

   "And the pig, though it has divided hooves, does not chew the cud; it is unclean for you."

   The pig is considered unclean and not fit for consumption.

   - *Regarding the term "horn" as rendered by Louis Segond in verse 7 of Leviticus, the Larousse dictionary provides the following definitions for the word "horn":*

   1. *A hard, pointed, and paired protrusion adorning the heads of certain mammals, serving as an offensive or defensive weapon.*

   2. *A substance (keratin) that constitutes superficial areas or hard organs (hoof, nail, claw, horn).*

The translation of this verse refers to the hoofs of animals' feet. This is the translation found in certain biblical versions:

- *v. 7 (The New Segond Bible): "The pig, which has split hooves and cloven feet, but does not chew the cud: it is unclean for you."*
- *v. 7 (The Bible in Everyday French): "The pig, because it has split hooves, but it does not chew the cud."*
- *v. 7 (La Colombe): "The pig, which has a split hoof and a cloven foot, but does not chew the cud: you will regard it as unclean."*

In addition to the Bible's explicit prohibition against the consumption of pork, here is, among many others, an opinion regarding its harmfulness to human health:

"The pig is subject to two (2) diseases that are unique to it: cysticercosis and swine fever. It is frequently attacked by trichinosis, quinsy (a type of tonsillitis), and anthrax or carbon. Pork meat swarms with parasites."—Pierre Larousse, Grand Universal Dictionary of the 19th Century, 1866

10. **What consequence does the Bible mention for those who eat pork?** *Isaiah 66:16-17*

"Those who consecrate and purify themselves to enter the gardens, following one in the midst, eating pork, vermin, and rats — they will all meet their end together, declares the Lord."

The passage makes it clear that God will judge those who eat things He has declared abominable, including pork.

11. **What does the Bible say about consuming blood?** *Leviticus 17:13-14; Acts 15:20*

The Bible strictly forbids the consumption of blood, requiring that the blood of all slaughtered animals be drained.

"For the life of every creature is its blood. That is why I have said to the Israelites: 'You must not eat the blood of any creature, because the life of every creature is its blood; anyone who eats it will be cut off.'" — Leviticus 17:14

"Instead, we should write to them to abstain from food polluted by idols, from sexual immorality, from the meat of strangled animals, and blood." — Acts 15:20

These passages indicate that the Word of God explicitly forbids the consumption of blood, which naturally includes animals that have been strangled. The blood of any slaughtered animal must be drained.

12. **What exhortation is given to those living in the last days? Luke 21:34**

"Be careful, or your hearts will be weighed down with carousing, drunkenness and the anxieties of life, and that day will close on you suddenly like a trap."

We must ensure that appetite and the worries of life do not prevent us from being ready for the return of Jesus.

13. **What principle should guide our way of living?** *1 Corinthians 10:31*

"So whether you eat or drink or whatever you do, do it all for the glory of God."

Our way of life, including how we care for our health, should be seen as an act of worship to God.

Recap : Reflection Questions drawn from this study

1. To whom does our body belong?

2. Can we destroy our bodies without consequences?

3. Name two factors that promote good health.

4. What diet was given to man in Eden?

5. According to the Bible, what characteristics make sea creatures fit for consumption?

6. What is said about the consumption of pork?

STUDY #18: SYSTEMATIC GENEROSITY

God created everything and, consequently, everything belongs to Him. But in managing earthly things, He always wants to associate us with Him; in this management, He always strives to remind us that He is the owner, and we are His managers or stewards. To mark His ownership or authority over what He gives us to manage, God always sets aside a portion that we, as managers, cannot appropriate for ourselves. He did this twice (2) in Eden, at creation. While allowing our first parents to enjoy everything in the garden, He reserves a part: the tree of the knowledge of good and evil; on the other hand, in creating the week, divided into seven parts or days, He reserves a portion of time: the seventh day.

It seems that throughout the ages, the Eternal has continued to reserve a portion of what we possess as the right to control our lives and our bodies. This study aims to clarify these points.

1. **To whom do all the riches of the earth belong? Haggai 2:8; Ps 50:10-12**

"The silver is mine, and the gold is mine, says the Lord of hosts" Haggai 2:8

"If I were hungry, I would not tell you; for the world is mine, and all that it contains"

- *All the riches of the earth belong to God who created them all. Everything we have and claim to possess (goods, health, talents) is nothing other than blessings received from God.*

2. **Where does the power that enables men to acquire wealth come from? Deut 8:17, 18**

"Beware of saying in your heart: 'My strength and the power of my hand have acquired these riches.' Remember the Lord your God, for it is He who gives you the power to get wealth, to confirm, as He does today, His covenant which He swore to your fathers"

- *The riches themselves, and the strength and talents to acquire them come from the Lord. We must manage them with humility and with feelings of gratitude.*

3. What portion of our income does God claim? Lev 27:30, 32

"Every tithe of the land, whether of the seed of the land or the fruit of the trees, belongs to the Lord; it is holy to the Lord." v. 30

- *The tithe is the tenth part of our income; it belongs to the Lord. That said, the tithe is not a gift we give to Him. Israel being a nation of farmers and shepherds, naturally drew its tithe from these activities. In different societies, throughout the ages, the tithe has remained the same: tenth part of income.*

4. For what purpose does God claim the tithe? Num 18:21; 1 Cor 9:13-14

"I give to the sons of Levi all the tithe in Israel as a possession, for their service which they perform, the service of the tent of meeting" Num 18:21 "Do you not know that those who perform sacred duties eat from the temple and those who serve at the altar share in the altar? In the same way, the Lord has commanded that those who preach the gospel should live from the gospel" 1 Cor 9:13-14

- *Among the twelve (12) tribes of Israel, the tribe of Levi was exclusively attached to sanctuary services. The Lord assigns them all tithes received in Israel in return for their service. During the New Testament period when the Levitical priesthood ended, the priestly function consisting of preaching the Gospel is fulfilled by those who devote themselves exclusively to these tasks. The tithe thus continues to fulfill the same role as in the Old Testament period. The apostle Paul emphasized this by declaring "Those who preach the Gospel should live from the Gospel"*

5. What severe reproaches does God address concerning unfaithfulness in paying tithe? Malachi 3:7-9

"Will a man rob God? Yet you rob me. But you say, 'How do we rob you?' In tithes and offerings. You are cursed with a curse, for you are robbing me, the whole nation" Mal 3:8, 9

- *This passage emphasizes that not paying one's tithe and offerings is robbing God or an act of unfaithfulness because the tithe belongs to the Lord. However, note the fundamental difference between tithe and offerings. While tithe represents the tenth part of our income, the level of offerings is voluntary; that is, determined by our degree of generosity and blessings received from the Lord. The Bible does not set a quota or percentage to apply to our offerings. In an address to Israel, on celebrating Passover, it is said: "Each shall give as he is able, according to the blessing of the Lord your God that he has given you" Deut 16:17. Nevertheless, this generosity should be systematic, meaning that each person sets for themselves the percentage of offering they want to always accompany their tithe.*

6. What special blessings are promised to those who are faithful in paying tithe? Mal 3:10-11

"Bring the full tithe into the storehouse, that there may be food in my house. Put me to the test, says the Lord of hosts, if I will not open the windows of heaven for you and pour out for you a blessing until there is no more need" Mal 3:10

7. In what terms does Jesus approve the payment of tithe? Matt 23:23

"Woe to you, scribes and Pharisees, hypocrites! For you tithe mint and dill and cumin, and have neglected the weightier matters of the law: justice and mercy and faithfulness. These you ought to have done, without neglecting the others"

- *By declaring: "these you ought to have done, without neglecting the others," Jesus recognizes and approves the validity and necessity of paying tithe. He wants to emphasize, however, that this practice must be done within the framework of a religious life marked by love, justice, mercy, and faithfulness. Any visible external act, like paying tithe, which is not the product of sincere piety, is mere formalism and, consequently, has no value before God.*

8. With what attitude should we give? 2 Cor 9:7, 8

"Each one must give as he has decided in his heart, not reluctantly or under compulsion, for God loves a cheerful giver" 2 Cor 9:7, 8

- *Our generosity and liberality toward the Lord must be done with joy, without constraint. This must be the expression of our love for God, for who He is, and what He does for us each day.*

RECAP: REFLECTION THEMES DRAWN FROM THIS STUDY

1. The definition of tithe
2. According to the Bible, to whom does it belong?
3. What do offerings represent?
4. In the Old Testament, what were tithes intended for?
5. Is tithe still in effect during the New Testament period?

STUDY #19: THE INVESTIGATIVE JUDGMENT

The Bible declares that we must all appear before God's tribunal and each will have to give account for himself (Rom 14:10, 12). In the context of an ordinary human judgment, we always imagine a criminal court sitting with at least: a judge, lawyers, witnesses, a prosecutor, an accused, clerks, and legal texts which are the basis of judgment. Generally, the accused appears personally before the Court to answer for the facts they are accused of. In God's judgment, will things happen the same way? Will Jesus, at His coming, set up a tribunal with all these arrangements where all men must appear personally at the bar? It seems not, when we remember Jesus' declaration: "Behold, I am coming soon, bringing my recompense with me, to repay each one for what he has done" Rev 22:12

Yes, Jesus returns to bring retributions, that is, the results of a judgment that will have been made before His second coming: The investigative judgment. What then are the components of this judgment?

1. **According to what principles will this judgment be carried out? Rev 20:12**

"And I saw the dead, great and small, standing before the throne. Books were opened... and the dead were judged according to their works, by what was written in the books"

- *This passage indicates that judgment will be made according to what is written in the books. There is no physical personal presence in this case.*

2. **How many books does the Bible mention?**

    a. The book of remembrance Mal 3:16

    b. The book of guilty actions (sins); Jer 2:22

    c. The book of life: Rev 3:5

3. **In whose presence are the books examined? Dan 7:9, 10**

"As I looked, thrones were placed, and the Ancient of Days took his seat; his clothing was white as snow, and the hair of his head like pure wool; his throne was fiery flames; its wheels were burning fire. The court sat in judgment, and the books were opened"

- *The examination of the books takes place in the presence of the Ancient of Days: the Father.*

4. **Who is the advocate or mediator? 1 John 2:1; 1 Tim 2:5; Matt 10:32, 33**

"My little children, I am writing these things to you so that you may not sin. But if anyone does sin, we have an advocate with the Father, Jesus Christ the righteous" 1 John 2:1

- *In the heavenly sanctuary, Jesus is our advocate and mediator. When we sin and confess our sins with a repentant heart, Jesus presents His pierced hands to the Father; and with the merits of His blood, He claims pardon on our behalf. We should all take advantage of His priestly ministry now while there is time. For the time will come when the door of grace will be closed; at that time, He will lay aside His advocate's garment to put on that of the judge.*

5. Who are the witnesses at this judgment? Heb 1:13, 14

"And to which of the angels has he ever said, 'Sit at my right hand'… Are they not all ministering spirits sent out to serve for the sake of those who are to inherit salvation?"

- *Angels are the witnesses at this judgment; witnesses of God's various calls inviting us to repentance and witnesses also of our refusal to accept this call.*

6. By what criteria will we be judged? James 2:10, 12

"So, speak and so act as those who are to be judged under the law of liberty" James 2:12

- *Liberty consists in doing what the law allows. The moral law, the decalogue, will be the basis of judgment, but the law in its entirety. Whoever disregards one of the Ten Commandments becomes guilty of all.*

7. Which class of people will be called first to judgment? 1 Peter 4:17

"For it is time for judgment to begin at the household of God. And if it begins with us, what will be the outcome for those who do not obey the gospel of God?"

- *Judgment must begin with God's people, the house of God. All those who profess to believe in God and obey His word are part of this group. Their cases will be examined first.*

8. What exhortation is made to us regarding this judgment? Ezek 18:23, 24

"Have I any pleasure in the death of the wicked, declares the Lord God, and not rather that he should turn from his way and live?" Ezek 18:23

- *To change conduct and live, such is God's will for all humans.*

9. **For the repentant sinner, what will happen to their name in the Book of life? Rev 3:5**

"The one who conquers will be clothed thus in white garments, and I will never blot his name out of the book of life. I will confess his name before my father and before his angels."

- *Their name will be written in the Book of Life.*

10. **In anticipation of judgment, what should be our duty? Eccl 12:15, 16**

"Fear God and keep his commandments, for this is the whole duty of man... For God will bring every deed into judgment, with every secret thing, whether good or evil"

11. **Is it sufficient to just start well in the Christian race? Matt 24:13; Heb 3:14**

"But the one who endures to the end will be saved" Matt 24:13

- *Given this judgment, we must examine ourselves daily to realize if we are still connected to Jesus. We must not only begin the race but must finish it. Let nothing in this world prevent us from responding to Jesus' call and holding fast to it until the end.*

RECAP: REFLECTION THEMES DRAWN FROM THIS STUDY:

1. Does God's tribunal sit with the physical presence of all men?
2. The main books of judgment
3. By what criteria will we be judged?

STUDY #20: THE TWO (2) COVENANTS

What is a covenant? The word covenant (from Hebrew, berith; from Greek, diatheke) means a formal agreement, a contract, or a treaty between two parties. In the Bible, God made several covenants: with individuals such as Noah (Gen 9:9-13) and Abraham (Gen 17:4-7). But two (2) covenants seem to have particular importance for God's people through the ages: The covenant made with Israel in the wilderness of Sinai, commonly called the First or Old Covenant, and another called the New Covenant. Many Christians believe we live under the New Covenant; they express a truth because it is by the prescripts of the Word of God. But unfortunately, they also come to think that being under the New Covenant releases Christians from the teachings of the Old Testament.

But what are, for the Christian, the consequences of being under the New Covenant? What is the content of these two covenants? This study aims to elucidate these points.

1. **What is the content of the covenant made with Israel or the First Covenant? Ex 19:5-8**

"Now therefore, if you will indeed obey my voice and keep my covenant, you shall be my treasured possession among all peoples, for all the earth is mine... Moses came and called the elders of the people and set before them all these words that the Lord had commanded him... All the people answered together and said, 'All that the Lord has spoken we will do.' Moses reported the words of the people to the Lord."

- *A contract generally requires the agreement of two parties. According to the terms of this covenant, the Lord commits to make Israel His people among all peoples of the earth, that is, a kingdom of priests, a holy nation. And Israel, in return, commits to obey and do "all that the Lord has said." From then on, the contract is perfect, the covenant is concluded: the First Covenant. The choice of Israel does not mean that God's oracles do not address other peoples of the earth; Israel should be His ambassador and spokesperson.*

2. **What special event sealed this First Covenant? Exodus 24:6-8**

"Moses took half of the blood and put it in basins, and half of the blood he threw against the altar... And Moses took the blood and threw it on the people and said, 'Behold the blood of the covenant that the Lord has made with you by all these words.'"

- *This covenant was marked and sealed by the shedding of blood, the blood of animals. Moses, through this office, already announces the priestly function that would later fall to Aaron's family.*

3. Who is concerned by this First Covenant? Gen 17:7

"And I will establish my covenant between me and you and your offspring after you throughout their generations for an everlasting covenant, to be God to you and your offspring after you"

- *This covenant is made with Abraham and his descendants throughout their generations. Through Isaac and Jacob, this covenant was to be perpetuated. Abraham's physical lineage thus represents the direct beneficiaries of this covenant, that is, Israel according to the flesh.*

4. What sign was to mark this First Covenant? Gen 17:10-12

"This is my covenant, which you shall keep, between me and you and your offspring after you: Every male among you shall be circumcised... It shall be a sign of the covenant between me and you"

- *Every male eight days old should be circumcised; this is a visible mark of the Lord's covenant with the people of Israel.*

5. Did Israel respect the terms of this covenant? Jer 32:21-23

"You brought your people Israel out of the land of Egypt... And they came in and took possession of it, but they did not obey your voice or walk in your law. They did nothing of all you commanded them to do. Therefore, you have made all this disaster come upon them"

- *Israel violated the terms of the agreement with the Lord, they disobeyed. The worship of the golden calf at the foot of Mount Sinai is the beginning of a long series of revolts and apostasies of the people who went so far as to worship the gods of the pagans. Israel many times provoked and irritated the Lord.*

6. Faced with Israel's failure, what promise is made by the Lord? Jer 31:31-32

"Behold, the days are coming, declares the Lord, when I will make a new covenant with the house of Israel and the house of Judah, not like the covenant that I made with their fathers on the day when

I took them by the hand to bring them out of the land of Egypt, my covenant that they broke, though I was their husband, declares the Lord"

- *The Lord thus announces the establishment of a new agreement, a new covenant with Israel; but this time, it will be with spiritual Israel which will include Jews and Gentiles.*

7. Who inaugurated the New Covenant? Heb 7:22; Heb 9:15

"This makes Jesus the guarantor of a better covenant" Heb 7:22 "Therefore he is the mediator of a new covenant" Heb 9:15

- *Jesus, through His death, becomes the mediator of the New Covenant.*

8. What are the similarities and differences between the Old and New Covenant?

1. The subjects or beneficiaries:

   a. **The Old Covenant concerns Israel according to the flesh,** that is, the physical descendants of Abraham, according to their generations: "God said to Abraham, 'As for you, you shall keep my covenant, you and your offspring after you throughout their generations'" Gen 17:9

   b. **The New Covenant includes converted Jews and Gentiles or pagans, accepted by adoption in the plan of salvation.** In this New Covenant, spiritual Israel or Israel by faith consists of all those who accept Jesus by faith:

"Know then that it is those of faith who are the sons of Abraham. And the Scripture, foreseeing that God would justify the Gentiles by faith, preached the gospel beforehand to Abraham, saying, 'In you shall all the nations be blessed.' So then, those who are of faith are blessed along with Abraham, the man of faith... And if you are Christ's, then you are Abraham's offspring, heirs according to promise" Gal 3:7-9, 29

"For no one is a Jew who is merely one outwardly, nor is circumcision outward and physical. But a Jew is one inwardly, and circumcision is a matter of the heart..." Rom 2:28, 29(a)

"Or is God the God of Jews only? Is he not the God of Gentiles also? Yes, of Gentiles also... since there is one God who will justify the circumcised by faith and the uncircumcised through faith" Rom 3:29

2. Shedding of blood

    a.   The First Covenant was sealed with the blood of animals: "For when every commandment of the law had been declared by Moses to all the people, he took the blood of calves and goats, with water and scarlet wool and hyssop, and sprinkled both the book itself and all the people, saying, 'This is the blood of the covenant that God commanded for you'" Heb 9:19, 20

    b.   The New Covenant is sealed with the blood of Jesus: "He entered once for all into the holy places, not using the blood of goats and calves but using his blood, thus securing an eternal redemption" Heb 9:1

3. Priesthood or sacrificial system

    a.   **The First Covenant is centered on the priestly ministry of the sacrifice** through whom the sinner approached God to obtain forgiveness of sin. Thus, the priest, a man, was the mediator.

          "And the anointed priest shall bring some of the blood of the bull into the tent of meeting" Lev 4:16

    b.   **Under the New Covenant, Jesus is the high priest (Heb 9:11):** "But as it is, Christ has obtained a ministry that is as much more excellent than the old as the covenant he mediates is better since it is enacted on better promises" Heb 8:6

4. **Obedience to the law**

   a. **In the First Covenant, God's laws are written on stone tablets and in books:**

   "When he had finished speaking with him on Mount Sinai, he gave Moses the two tablets of the testimony, tablets of stone, written with the finger of God" Exodus 31:18

   "All the people gathered as one man into the square before the Water Gate. And they told Ezra the scribe to bring the Book of the Law of Moses that the Lord had commanded Israel" Nehemiah 8:1

   b. **In the New Covenant, God's laws are rather written in hearts and minds, thus showing their permanence.** Obedience to God's law is always at the heart of the relationship between God and man whether in the Old or New Covenant: "This is the covenant that I will make with them after those days, declares the Lord: I will put my laws on their hearts, and write them on their minds" Heb 10:16

5. **Excellence and duration**

   a. **The First Covenant was not perfect and therefore obsolete:**

   "For if that first covenant had been faultless, there would have been no occasion to look for a second... In speaking of a new covenant, he makes the first one obsolete. And what is becoming obsolete and growing old is ready to vanish away" Heb 8:7, 13

b. **The New Covenant is superior and more excellent than the firs**t: "But as it is, DRAWNChrist has obtained a ministry that is as much more excellent than the old as the covenant he mediates is better, since it is enacted on better promises" Heb 8:6

In summary, the First Covenant opened the way to the second; and the latter is more inclusive because it includes all humans, Jews and Gentiles, without distinction of race and origin. Let us thank God for this salvation and let us all take advantage of it!

RECAP: REFLECTION THEMES DRAWN FROM THIS STUDY

1. What does the word "Covenant" mean?
2. With whom was the First Covenant made?
3. With whom is the New Covenant made?
4. What is the relationship of God's law with the two Covenants?
5. Similarities and differences between the two Covenants

STUDY #21: THE VISION OF THE FOUR BEASTS

The theme under study could also be titled: "God unveils the future." Men have always claimed to reveal the future through Chiromancy. However, the Bible teaches us that only God can predict the future, and this with amazing accuracy. Nations and empires emerge, know glory, and disappear according to the plan previously traced by God. In a vision given to King Nebuchadnezzar in chapter two of the book of Daniel (Daniel 2:1-49), God reveals, through the metallic parts of a statue, the symbols of empires or kingdoms that should succeed each other in human history. The culminating point of this prophecy is noted in the following passage: "A stone was cut out by no human hand, and it struck the image on its feet of iron and clay and broke them in pieces... But the stone that struck the image became a great mountain and filled the whole earth" Daniel 2:34, 35(b). God further illuminates the symbol of this stone by saying: "And in the days of those kings the God of heaven will set up a kingdom that shall never be destroyed, nor shall the kingdom be left to another people. It shall break in pieces all these kingdoms and bring them to an end, and it shall stand forever" Daniel 2:44.

In chapter 7 of the book of Daniel, God gives the prophet a vision: "The Vision of the Four Beasts" which covers the same reality, and the same message as chapter 2, but this time under the symbols of living beings: animals. It should be noted that this second vision is not a simple replica or exact reproduction of the statue vision in Daniel 2. The major difference between the two is that the vision of the beasts gives more details or further deepens the symbols relating to the different kingdoms. The point of similarity is that both culminate in the same event: the eternal reign of Jesus' kingdom. "And the kingdom and the dominion and the greatness of the kingdoms under the whole heaven shall be given to the people of the saints of the Highest; his kingdom shall be an everlasting kingdom, and all dominions shall serve and obey him" Daniel 7:27.

The objective of this theme: "The Vision of the Four Beasts", is to remind us once again that:

1. God predicts and reveals the course of history through the Bible.

2. We must prepare ourselves for the great event of Jesus' return.

1. How does the vision of the four beasts begin? Daniel 7:1-3 "

"In the first year of Belshazzar king of Babylon, Daniel had a dream and visions of his head" Daniel 7:1

"Daniel declared, 'I saw in my vision by night, and behold, the four winds of heaven were stirring up the great sea'" Daniel 7:2

"And four great beasts came up out of the sea, different from one another" Daniel 7:3

- Belshazzar (literally: Bel-Shar-Usur) was the eldest son of King Nabonidus and the latter (Nabonidus) was Nebuchadnezzar's son-in-law.

- Explanation of the two symbols: winds and sea (water)

- In biblical prophecy "winds" signify "war, conflict" (Jer 49:36, 37)

- The Bible uses sea or waters to symbolize peoples, nations, and multitudes (Rev 17:15; Isaiah 17:12, 13)

- The winds denote battles and wars. It is through them that kingdoms rise and fall.

- The great sea is the symbol of the mass of humanity, especially pagan humanity within which various empires are formed.

2. What do these beasts symbolize? Daniel 7:17

"These four great beasts are four kings who shall arise out of the earth"

- In this prophecy of Daniel 7, the word king is also translated as "kingdom". "Thus, he said: 'The fourth beast shall be a fourth kingdom on earth'" Daniel 7:23. These four great beasts symbolize four kingdoms or empires that should arise from the earth.

- One can see a comparison or parallelism between Nebuchadnezzar's vision in chapter 2 and Daniel's in chapter 7. In Chapter 2, the kingdoms are symbolized by metals presented in decreasing order of value (gold, silver, brass, iron). In chapter 7, they are symbolized by beasts presented in decreasing order of power and strength (lion, bear, leopard).

3. What does the first beast (the lion) symbolize? Daniel 7:4

"The fit was like a lion and had eagles' wings. Then as I looked its wings were plucked off, and it was lifted from the ground and made to stand on two feet like a man, and the mind of a man was given to it"

The lion represents the empire of Babylon which reigned over the world from 606 to 538 BC.

The lion is a well-suited symbol for Babylon. King of Beasts, it corresponds to the head of gold of the statue (gold is the king of metals) and describes the mighty reign of Babylon. As for the swiftness of this beast symbolized by its eagle's wings, history reports that in thirty years, Nebuchadnezzar conquered Arabia, Egypt, Judea, and Syria. "The symbol of the lion is typical of Babylon, especially in the time of Nebuchadnezzar, when the Ishtar Gate was decorated on each side with a long procession of yellow lions on a background of blue ceramics, in relief, overhanging" The Expositor's Bible Commentary, Vol. 7, p. 85-86, 1985

- The words "its wings were plucked off" can apply either to the temporary punishment inflicted on Nebuchadnezzar (Dan 4:24-27), or to the capture of Babylon by the Medes in 538 during which Belshazzar, Nebuchadnezzar's grandson, was killed (Dan 5:25-31).

- The new posture of the lion: "Made to stand on two feet like a man" and the "mind of a man was given to it," foreshadowed less cruel, thus more human behavior evoked in 2 Kings 25:27-30

4. What does the second beast (the Bear) symbolize? Dan 7:5

"And behold another beast, a second one, like a bear. It was raised on one side. It had three ribs in its mouth between its teeth; and it was told, 'Arise, devour much flesh'"

- The bear represents the Medo-Persian empire which reigned from 538 to 331 BC

In Daniel chapter 2, the silver of the chest and arms is inferior to the head of gold; likewise, the bear is inferior to the lion. The Medo-Persian empire was inferior to Babylon in terms of riches, magnificence, and splendor.

- The fact that this animal was raised on one side means that the Persians were stronger than the Medes in their federation. This image corresponds well to that of the ram which had one horn higher than the other (Dan 8:3).

- The three ribs seen in the bear's mouth are generally interpreted as an allusion to the great conquests of the Persian empire: Lydia, Babylon, and Egypt.

5. What does the third beast (The leopard) symbolize? Dan 7:6

"After this I looked, and behold, another, like a leopard, with four wings of a bird on its back. And the beast had four heads, and dominion was given to it"

- The leopard represents the Greek empire which reigned from 331 to 168 BC

In Daniel's Vision chapter 2, there is a degradation; that is, the brass of the thighs is inferior to the silver of the chest and arms, likewise, the leopard is inferior to the bear. The Greek empire was inferior to the Medo-Persians in terms of moral values.

- The leopard is known for its flexibility and agility; this is why it is seen with four wings on its back, an unusual number. This translates to a greater speed than that indicated about Babylon. The leopard's wings indicate its extraordinary speed and extension. In twelve years, Alexander the Great extended his empire to the banks of the Indus. His victories resembled lightning wars.
- At the death of the conqueror, his kingdom was divided among his generals. The four heads of the leopard represent the four generals who would share the territory:
  1. Seleucus, in the East (Territory of Syria)
  2. Lysimachus, in the North (Territory of Thrace)
  3. Cassander, in the West (Territory of Macedonia)
  4. Ptolemy, in the South (Territory of Egypt)

6. What does the fourth beast (The terrible beast) symbolize? Dan 7:7

"After this, I saw in the night visions, and behold, a fourth beast, terrifying and dreadful and exceedingly strong. It had great iron teeth; it devoured and broke in pieces and stamped what was left with its feet.

It was different from all the beasts that were before it, and it had ten horns"

- The fourth beast represents the Roman Empire (168 BC - 476 AD). It corresponds to the iron legs of the statue in Daniel 2. Iron aptly symbolizes the Roman Empire where everything was indeed made of iron: its army, its methods, and its strategies. All this well reflects the ferocity of this terrible beast described in verse 7. During the inauguration of the Colosseum in Rome, it was reported that no less than five thousand animals and two thousand gladiators were sacrificed.

7. What do the ten horns of the beast symbolize?

"It had ten horns... The ten horns are ten kings who shall arise from this kingdom" Dan 7:7, 24

- The ten horns represent ten kingdoms that emerged from the Roman Empire. At the end of the fifth century, barbarians invaded and dismantled the Roman Empire and, from its ruins, emerged ten (10) nations of Western Europe. The last Roman emperor, Romulus Augustulus, was dethroned in 476 by the barbarian king Odoacer.

The ten (10) kingdoms of Western Europe:
Anglo-Saxons - Great Britain
Franks – France
Alamanni – Germany
Burgundians – Switzerland
Lombards – Italy
Ostrogoths – Destroyed
Vandals – Destroyed
Suevi – Portugal
Heruli – Destroyed
Visigoths - Spain

Despite multiple attempts at political alliances made during fifteen centuries and treaties or marriages between sovereigns of different countries, they never managed to rebuild an empire; all this to confirm Daniel's predictions: "but they will not adhere to one another, just as iron does not mix with clay" Daniel 2:43

Comparative Table of the Two Visions (Daniel 2 and Daniel 7)

Empires -	Daniel 2 (Symbols) -	Daniel 7 (Symbols) -	Periods
1. Babylon	Gold	Leo	606-538 BC
2. Medo-Persia	Silver	Bear	538-331 BC
3. Greece	Brass	Leopard	331-168 BC
4. Rome	Iron	Terrible Beast	168 BC-476 AD
5. The 10 Kind. Iron and Clay (the 10 Toes) The 10 Horns (Little Horn)			476 AD

8. How did God predict the fall of these empires and the establishment of an eternal kingdom? Dan 7:13, 14, 18, 27

"I saw in the night visions, and behold, with the clouds of heaven there came one like a son of man, and he came to the Ancient of Days and was presented before him... And to him was given dominion and glory and a kingdom, that all peoples, nations, and languages should serve him; his dominion is an everlasting dominion, which shall not pass away, and his kingdom one that shall not be destroyed" Dan 7:13,14

The prophecies of Daniel 2 and 7 deliver the same message to humanity: God controls the events of history and will have the last word. Like these universal empires that succeeded one another, nations have formed on the face of the earth, some more powerful than others, but they are all called to disappear to see the establishment of an eternal kingdom that Jesus will come to establish upon His return. Now is the time for all men to make a choice: the choice to obey the Savior's voice and confirm their place in this eternal kingdom. It is more than ever the time to think about it according to what is said in Hebrews 4:7: "God again sets a day, 'Today,' saying through David so long afterward, as has been said before, 'Today, if you hear his voice, do not harden your hearts.'"

RECAP: REFLECTION THEMES DRAWN FROM THIS STUDY

1. Name the four beasts seen by Daniel and recall their prophetic significance. Recall the periods of reign of:

   a. The Babylonian Empire

b. The Medo-Persian Empire

c. The Greek Empire

d. The Roman Empire

2. How many barbarian tribes invaded and dismantled the Roman Empire?

3. Name the four generals who shared the Greek empire after Alander the Great's death.

STUDY #22: THE LITTLE HORN OR THE MYSTERIOUS POWER

The dominant point of the visions of Daniel 2 and 7 is the outcome of world history characterized, on one hand, by the little stone that must strike the feet of the statue to destroy all world powers and establish an eternal kingdom (Dan 2); on the other hand, the fact that "the kingdom and dominion and the greatness of the kingdoms under the whole heaven shall be given to the people of the saints of the Highest" (Dan 7). The vision of the four beasts introduces new concepts: ten horns and a little horn. This little horn seems to dominate Daniel's vision both by the multiplicity of its activities and by the depth and consequences of its actions. "I considered the horns, and behold, there came up among them another horn, a little one, before which three of the first horns were plucked up by the roots. And behold, in this horn were eyes like the eyes of a man, and a mouth speaking great things" Dan 7:8

What then is the prophetic and historical meaning of this little horn? How to identify it through its characteristics? This is the objective of the present study which will focus on the main points characterizing this little horn that we also designate as a mysterious power.

1. Its origin: Daniel 7:8

"A little horn came up among them."

* *This power should come up from among the ten horns which themselves represent the different states that succeeded the*

dismantling of the Roman empire. Thus, having come out of Rome, the fourth empire, the Papacy or religious Rome well answers the characteristics expressed in Daniel's vision. The little horn effectively came up from among the horns.

2. Difference from other powers: Daniel 7:24

"Another shall arise after them; he shall be different from the first ones"

- *Temporal powers have always confined themselves to activities related to their role, thus designating their ambassadors in countries where they are represented. The Papacy is a power different from others, that is, politico-religious. The Vatican has its representative, the Apostolic Nuncio, in the states of the world just like ambassadors from other countries.*

3. Its intolerance: Humbling of three kings: Daniel 7:8, 24

"And three of the first horns were plucked up by the roots before it... The ten horns are ten kings who shall arise from this kingdom. Another shall arise after them; he shall be different from the first ones and shall put down three kings"

To ensure absolute power, the Papacy annihilated three nations that had emerged from the ruins of the Roman empire by treating them as heretics.

"At the time when the barbarians were settling in the empire, some of them such as the Heruli, the Vandals, and the Ostrogoths, were already baptized, not in the great Catholic Church, but in the faith of the Arians. The Arians, led by the Alexandrian priest Arius, denied the divinity of Jesus. This constituted one of the greatest heresies in the eyes of the Papacy. Faced with the danger of religious contamination posed by the presence of these heretics within Christianity, the Papacy could only wish to eliminate such an obstacle. Very quickly, this hope would soon be realized. These three Arian powers (the Heruli, the Vandals, the Ostrogoths) would be annihilated and evicted from the Roman empire under the direct instigation of the papacy, in full agreement with Daniel's prediction: "Three of the first horns were plucked up by the roots before it; The Heruli in 493 AD, The Vandals in

534 AD, and the Ostrogoths in 538 AD". (Daniel-Rops L'Église des Temps Barbares, p.133-134, Paris,1950)

4. Its arrogance

"It had eyes like the eyes of a man, and a mouth speaking great things" Daniel 7:8

"I looked then because of the sound of the great words that the horn was speaking" Daniel 7:11

"He shall speak words against the Highest" Daniel 7:25

- *Through notes and declarations taken from works written by Catholic authors, one well understands that arrogance is the main characteristic of the papacy. Here are some:*

  1. **"To attribute to creatures exclusively divine prerogatives is to blaspheme".** Dictionary of Catholic Theology, A. Vacant and E. Mangenot, Paris, 1905

  2. **"...So great is the dignity and elevation of the pope that he is not simply a man, but almost God.... "...Thus, by a triple crown, the pope is consecrated king of heaven, earth, and hell.**

     "He indeed possesses such dignity and power that he constitutes with Christ the same judicial authority.... "...One must have recourse to the authority of the pope; the pope is in some way God on earth, the only head of Christians, the supreme king of all kings, who possesses the fullness of power and to whom the almighty God has given the government of his earthly and celestial empire" Lucius Ferrari, Prompta biblioteca, Venice, 1763, p. 17, 18

5. War against the saints: Daniel 7:25

"He shall wear out the saints of the Highest"

- *"The Roman Catholic Church has, for centuries, persecuted all those who went against its teachings. It treated them as heretics. "The Catholic Church resorts to force, corporal punishments, torture; it creates tribunals like those of the Inquisition; if needed it unleashes the crusade, the holy war, the war of religion.... This is what it did notably in the 16th century regarding Protestants; ... It lit in Italy, the Netherlands, and especially in Spain, the fires of the Inquisition; in France, under Francis I and Henry II; in England, under Mary Tudor, it tortured heretics". The Catholic Church, The Renaissance, Protestantism, Paris, 1905, p. 240-241.*

• *"It is in Spain that the inquisition raged in the worst way. In the city of Seville alone 4000 people were burned in forty years; until 1783, the number of burned is estimated at 31,000 people". Hans King, The Church p. 342-345.*

6. Change of times and law

"He shall think to change the times and the law" Daniel 7:25

The Decalogue (the ten commandments) is the only text of the Bible written by the finger of God (Exodus 31:18); all other parts of the Sacred Book were written by prophets inspired, certainly, by God (2 Peter 1:21). Considering God's law recorded in the doctrine and practice of the Church such innovations as: the mediation of saints, the mediation of priests, the sacrifice of the mass, confession in Exodus 20:2-17, we can see that it has been changed by the Roman Church. Below is the modified text:

The Ten Commandments of God:

1. You shall adore one God alone, and love Him perfectly.
2. You shall not swear by God in vain, nor by anything else.
3. You shall keep the Sundays, serving God devoutly.
4. You shall honor your father and mother, that you may live long.
5. You shall not be a murderer, in deed nor willingly.
6. You shall not be unchaste, in body or by consent.
7. You shall not take nor keep another's goods knowingly.
8. You shall not bear false witness, nor lie in any way.
9. You shall not desire carnal pleasure, except in marriage only.

10. You shall not desire others' goods, to have them unjustly. *(The Catechism of the Ecclesiastical Provinces of Que. Mtl and Otta, 1944, p. 9)*

- The following remarks should be made:

1. The statement of the divine text has been completely changed.

2. The second commandment, dealing with the making and worship of graven images, has been eliminated.

3. The fourth commandment relating to the Sabbath, the seventh day of the week, is replaced by "You shall keep the Sundays."

4. The tenth commandment dealing with covetousness has been split in two, just to compensate for the second commandment that was eliminated and thus maintain the number of ten commandments.

This position is clearly expressed through the following declarations:

1. **"The pope holds such great authority and power that he can modify, explain or interpret even divine laws".** Papa II, p. 18

2. **"In the catechisms, God's law has been changed and virtually promulgated by the papacy: The second commandment which forbids the making and worship of images is omitted, and the tenth which forbids coveting is divided in two".** *(Review & Herald Pub. Assoc., 1942), p. 221*

3. *"The authority of the Church is highlighted to the highest degree by the Scriptures since it recommends them, declares them divine, and delivers them for our reading... The Sabbath day of the law that we celebrate is transferred to the Lord's [Day]... This precept, as well as other similar articles, have not ended by Christ's teaching (he indeed said he came to fulfill the law and not to abolish it), but have been changed by the authority of the Church".* **Sacrorum Conciliorum Nova et amplissima Collectio, Paris-Leipzig, 1902**

7. Attack on Christ's priestly ministry: Daniel 8:9-12

"Out of one of them came a little horn... It grew great, even to the host of heaven. And some of the host and some of the stars it threw down to the ground and trampled on them. It took away the regular burnt offering... And the regular burnt offering was taken away... It threw truth to the ground, and it prospered in its doing"

Here are the declarations of God's Word relating to Christ's ministry:

"For there is one God, and there is one mediator between God and men, the man Christ Jesus". 1 Tim 2:5

"Consequently, he can save to the uttermost those who draw near to God through him, since he always lives to make intercession for them". Hebrews 7:25. By introducing into Church doctrine and practice innovations such as the mediation of saints, the mediation of priests, the sacrifice of the mass, confession auricular confession, the papacy has successfully caused the disappearance of the knowledge of Christ's priestly ministry in the heavenly sanctuary.

8. Duration of its supremacy

"He shall wear out the saints of the Highest... and they shall be given into his hand for a time, times, and half a time" Daniel 7:25

- The Jerusalem Bible version renders the verse thus: "And the saints shall be given into his hand for a time, two times, and half a time."

- This indicates the period during which the little horn should exercise its power. It should be remembered that in the prophecies described in certain books of the Bible (Daniel and Revelation), people, animals, and things often have symbolic value, for example: woman (virgin or prostitute), beast, horn, little horn, etc.

- The meaning of a prophetic "time": A prophetic time corresponds to a year of 360 days. The Hebrew word "iddam" translated as time and found in Daniel 4:16, 23, 25, 32 is synonymous with "year". From this, we can establish the duration indicated in the prophecy:

$$1 \text{ Time} = 1 \text{ year} = \quad 360 \text{ days}$$
$$2 \text{ Times} = 2 \text{ years} = 720 \text{ days}$$
$$\tfrac{1}{2} \text{ Time} = \tfrac{1}{2} \text{ year} = \quad 180 \text{ days}$$
$$\text{Total} = 1{,}260 \text{ days}$$

- The meaning of a prophetic day:

A prophetic day corresponds to one (1) literal year.

"I assign you a day for each year." Ezekiel 4:5, 6

"Everyone knows that a day is a year in prophetic style." (Antoine Court de Gebelin, Primitive World, p. 90, Paris 1781)

Consequently, the duration of the dominion or supremacy of the little horn is 1,260 years and not 1,260 literal days.

- **When does this period of 1,260 years begin and end?**

"In 533, Emperor Justinian (Roman) made a decree naming the Bishop of Rome the head of all churches. A few months later, he gave him the title of corrector of heretics. But these decrees did not take effect until the fall of the Ostrogoths, five (5) years later in 538 AD. This is why this year (538) is considered the beginning of papal domination. This supremacy ended in 1798 when Pope Pius VI was taken prisoner by the French General Berthier who took him into exile in France where he died" Jean Leflon, History of the Church from its origins to our days, p. 155-157, 1949.

9. **Other biblical symbols identify this power.**

The prophecies of Daniel and Revelation often contain common symbols presented under different names. Such is the case with the prophecy of the little horn treated in Daniel chapter 7. Revelation 13 takes up, under the features of a "beast rising from the sea" the same characteristics noted in the book of Daniel relating to the little horn (arrogance, blasphemy, personal elevation, duration of dominion, etc.)

The following biblical passages confirm it:

"But the woman was given the two wings of the great eagle so that she might fly from the serpent into the wilderness, to the place where she is to be nourished for a time, and times, and half a time" Rev 12:14

"And it was given a mouth speaking great things and blasphemies, and it was allowed to exercise authority for forty-two months...And it opened its mouth to utter blasphemies against God, to blaspheme his name and his dwelling, that is, those who dwell in heaven." Rev 13:5, 6

It should be noted that the period of forty-two months (42 x 30 = 1260), cited in Revelation 13, equals 1260 prophetic days or 1260 years, corresponding to the same period: a time, times, and half a time.

10. Recommendations and exhortations of God's Word

"I know that after my departure fierce wolves will come in among you, not sparing the flock; and from among yourselves will arise men speaking twisted things, to draw away the disciples after them." Acts 20:29, 30

"Let no one deceive you in any way. For that day will not come, unless the rebellion comes first, and the man of lawlessness is revealed, the son of destruction, who opposes and exalts himself against every so-called god or object of worship, so that he takes his seat in the temple of God, proclaiming himself to be God." 2 Thess 2:3, 4

"And the scribes and the Pharisees began to question, saying, 'Who is this who speaks blasphemies? Who can forgive sins but God alone?'" Luke 5:21

RECAP: REFLECTION THEMES DRAWN FROM THIS STUDY:

1. Its origin
2. Difference from other powers
3. Its intolerance
4. Its arrogance
5. War against the saints

6. Change of the law

7. Attack on Christ's priestly ministry

8. Duration of its supremacy

STUDY #23: THE BIBLE AND TRADITION

The Bible is God's inspired Word contained in the sixty-six (66) books (from Genesis to Revelation). Throughout history, men have introduced into Christianity doctrines that the Bible does not recognize or that are in flagrant contradiction with its teachings: tradition. It should be noted that tradition is a long and slow process that began in the first century of the Christian era. Jesus himself was often very severe, castigating his contemporaries who tried to replace the prescripts of God's Word with their traditions. "You leave the commandment of God and hold to the tradition of men" Mark 7:6. The objective of this study is to specify some points of traditions introduced into Christianity throughout history, to enlighten sincere souls who want to obey God.

1. **Since when did men try to introduce tradition into the Church? Matt 15:3, 8-9**

"He answered them, 'And why do you break the commandment of God for the sake of your tradition? These people honor me with their lips, but their heart is far from me; in vain do they worship me, teaching as doctrines the commandments of men'"

- *Jesus' rebuke to the Scribes and Pharisees means that, already in his time, they were trying to introduce tradition into the Church.*

2. **Against what is the Christian warned? Col 2:8**

"See to it that no one takes you captive by philosophy and empty deceit, according to human tradition and not according to Christ".

- *This exhortation from Paul to the Colossians is valid and applicable to Christians of all times and all ages.*

3. Some points of tradition introduced into the Church throughout history.

3.1 The worship of images: Exodus 20:4, 5

"You shall not make for yourself a carved image, or any likeness of anything that is in heaven above, or that is in the earth beneath, or that is in the water under the earth. You shall not bow down to them or serve them"

- *This second commandment of the decalogue expressly forbids all men, not only from making carved images but also from bowing down before them to worship them. The introduction of these images into the Church, as representing beings who at one time led a life of piety, is in flagrant opposition to the prescripts of God's Word.*

3.2 The cult of the dead: Eccl 9:5, 6

"For the living know that they will die, but the dead know nothing, and they have no more reward, for the memory of them is forgotten. Their love and their hate and their envy have already perished, and forever they have no more share in all that is done under the sun"

- *Practiced in pagan antiquity, the cult of the dead was introduced into Church doctrine, in defiance of this formal declaration of God's Word: "The dead know nothing". The cult of the dead rests on the theory of the immortality of the soul according to which, at death, an immaterial part called soul or spirit detaches from the body and continues to live by itself.*

3.3 - Intercession and mediation: Acts 4:12; 1 Tim 2:5; Heb 7:25

"For there is one God, and there is one mediator between God and men, the man Christ Jesus" 1 Tim 2:5 "There is salvation in no one else" Acts 4:12 "Consequently, he can save to the uttermost those who draw near to God through him since he always lives to make intercession for them" Heb 7:25

- *These passages show unequivocally that Jesus is the one and only mediator between God and men. Jesus, as intercessor, is the only means by which we are pardoned and saved. According to Catholic doctrine, saints are beings who lead exemplary lives on earth and, after their death, are declared saints, living in God's presence in heaven, consequently able to intercede with God on behalf of men. Furthermore, in 1215 AD, the Roman Church at the Fourth Lateran Council decreed and established auricular Confession according to which the faithful must confess to a priest to obtain forgiveness of their sins or absolution. In summary, these points of tradition (worship of saints and auricular confession), introduced into Church practice, disagree with the Bible for three reasons:*

1. They attack Jesus' mediatorial work who is the only mediator between God and men.

2. They promote the worship of images in violation of the 2nd commandment of the Decalogue.

3. They are centered on the cult of the dead

3.4 - Baptism by sprinkling or of children: Mark 16:16; Mark 1:9, 10

"Whoever believes and is baptized will be saved, but whoever does not believe will be condemned" Mark 16:16 "Jesus came from Nazareth of Galilee and was baptized by John in the Jordan... And when he came up out of the water, he saw the heavens being torn open" Mark 1:9, 10

These passages show that baptism is the result of belief and repentance. Baptism is the public manifestation of this belief, which a baby or child cannot do. Moreover, baptism symbolizes death with Jesus, and resurrection, to lead him to a new life. The word baptism comes from the Greek "baptizo" (to plunge, to immerse); there is no baptism without immersion; that is why Jesus, always wanting to be our example, was baptized in the Jordan by John.

"He came up out of the water," v.10, is a way of saying that he had gone down into the water. Only baptism by immersion conforms to the symbolism of death and resurrection. Baptism by a sprinkling of children disagrees with evangelical baptism.

3.5 - The day of rest: Exodus 20:8-11

"Remember the Sabbath day, to keep it holy... Six days you shall labor and do all your work, but the seventh day is a Sabbath to the Lord your God"

- *The rest (Sabbath), established by God at creation and recalled in the 4th commandment of the Decalogue obligates all men to rest. The Sabbath was made for man (Mark 2:27), that is, for all men without distinction of race or origin. However, in the 4th century of the Christian era, human tradition replaced the Lord's Day of rest with the sun's day of the astrological week, which became the Lord's Day. No verse of the New Testament dealing with the first day of the week suggested such a change.*

4. What call is made to sincere Christians? Rev 18:4; John 10:16

"Come out of her, my people, lest you take part in her sins, lest you share in her plagues" Rev 18:4 "And I have other sheep that are not of this fold. I must bring them also, and they will listen to my voice. So, there will be one flock, one shepherd" John 10:16

While Babylon is physically one of the four universal empires that ruled the world (from 606 to 538 BC), Babylon spiritually symbolizes confusion or any religious system that mixes truth and human traditions. The apostle John's call is solemn: "Come out of her, my people". This call must be heard and accepted by every sincere soul, for Jesus indeed said he has other sheep that must enter his fold to have life.

5. What was predicted concerning false teachers? 2 Peter 2:1-2
"

But false prophets also arose among the people, just as there will be false teachers among you, who will secretly bring in destructive heresies, even denying the Master who bought them, bringing upon themselves swift destruction. And many will follow their sensuality, and because of them the way of truth will be blasphemed"

- *God's Word predicted that truth would be slandered.*

6. What will be the fate of those who counterfeit God's Word? Rev 22:18, 19 "

I warn everyone who hears the words of the prophecy of this book: if anyone adds to them, God will add to him the plagues described in this book" Rev 22:18

- *These passages indicate that it is not without consequence that men take the initiative to add to or take away from God's Word.*

7. Whom should we obey? Acts 5:28, 29

"We must obey God rather than men"

- *It is God whom we must obey. Salvation is personal and individual. Neither parents nor society should in any way influence our decision to serve God.*

8. When should we decide to serve God? Heb 3:7, 8

"Today, if you hear his voice, do not harden your hearts"

- *It is today, the day of salvation, not tomorrow.*

RECAP: REFLECTION THEMES DRAWN FROM THIS STUDY:

1. Did tradition already exist in Jesus' time?
2. Recall, with biblical references, the five (5) points of tradition:

- Cult of the dead
- Worship of images
- Baptism by sprinkling
- Intercession and mediation
- Day of rest

Reminder of some dates of traditions introduced into Christianity:

Year	Event
160 AD	Beginning of Sunday observance
186	Doctrine of immortality of the soul
190	First prayers for the dead
220	Sign of the cross began
270	Introduction of baptism by sprinkling
321	Constantine's decree making Sunday observance mandatory
325	Council of Nicaea reinforcing Constantine's decree (of 321)
350	Christmas feast fixed to December 25
380	Emperor Theodosius's decree establishing the Catholic Church as a state religion
381	Primacy of the Bishop of Rome
538	Papal supremacy (Bishop of Rome declared head of all churches)
600	Latin introduced in worship
788	Worship of cross, images; relics of Saints
965	Baptism of bells
995	First canonization of Saint: Pope John XV canonized Ulrick, Bishop of Augsburg
1000	Mandatory celibacy of priests
1160	Doctrine of seven (7) sacraments
1190	Sale of indulgences
1215	Auricular confession
1215	Transubstantiation
1264	Feast of Corpus Christi officially established
1336	Procession of the Holy Sacrament
1415	Suppression of the Cup to the faithful
1439	Purgatory officially recognized
1545	Council of Trent declares tradition equal to Bible
1546	Apocryphal books added to Bible
1884	Immaculate Conception of Holy Virgin Mary

1870	Papal infallibility
1950	Assumption of Holy Virgin Mary
2003	Beatification of Sister Teresa

STUDY #24: JESUS AND THE CHURCH

The word 'Church' comes from Greek (EKKLESIA=called out); This word is used especially in the New Testament, but the concept "Church" is present in the Old Testament: it is God's people through the ages, passing through Noah, Shem, Abraham, Isaac, Jacob, or Israel. But a fundamental difference must be emphasized between the Church of the Old Testament and that of the New. The Church of the New Testament or Jesus's Church has a universal character and is in no way tied to national, racial, and ethnic boundaries. It includes Jews and Gentiles without distinction. "If you are Christ's, then you are Abraham's offspring, heirs according to promise" Gal 3:29.

Jesus's Church is the community of Christians, without reference to the notion of religion, which came long after in human history. That said, two important questions must be asked: 1- What are Jesus's relationships with this Church? 2- What consequences does this imply for Christians who claim to be disciples of Christ?

The present study intends to provide answers.

1. What are Jesus's relationships with the Church?

1.1 Jesus: Head of the Church: Ephesians 1:22, 23

"And he put all things under his feet and gave him as head over all things to the church, which is his body, the fullness of him who fills all in all"

- *This passage indicates that the Church is a body of which Jesus is the head or chief. In the human body, it's the head or brain that gives orders and the members obey. A member that doesn't obey impulses from the head would cease to be part of this body. It's the same for the Church; it's through obedience to Jesus that we demonstrate our affiliation with his Church. This is moreover what the Apostle John declares:*

"And by this, we know that we have come to know him if we keep his commandments. Whoever says 'I know him' but does not keep his commandments is a liar, and the truth is not in him… whoever says he abides in him ought to walk in the same way in which he walked" 1 John 2:3-4, 6

1.2 Jesus: Foundation of the Church: 1 Cor 3:9, 11; Eph 2:20

"For we are God's fellow workers. You are God's field, God's building… For no one can lay a foundation other than that which is laid, which is Jesus Christ" 1 Cor 3:9,11

"Built on the foundation of the apostles and prophets, Christ Jesus himself being the cornerstone" Eph 2:20

- The Church is represented by the image of a building of which Jesus is the foundation and cornerstone. This means that all Church teachings must be based on those of Jesus. Furthermore, Paul emphasizes that this foundation is unique and the only one. Some Christians, interpreting Matt 16:18 "You are Peter, and on this rock, I will build my church," wrongly conclude that the Church is built on the Apostle Peter.

The explanation of this verse is as follows:

- Peter (from Greek Petros): The Apostle Peter
- rock (from Greek petra): stone
- Jesus: the stone, the rock of ages (Isaiah 28:16)

"Therefore, thus says the Lord God, 'Behold, I am laying in Zion for a foundation a stone, a tested stone, a precious cornerstone, of a sure foundation: 'Whoever believes will not be in haste'"

- *The Church is not founded on Peter, but on Jesus, the cornerstone, the rock of ages. Moreover, Peter, as a man, showed his weakness like all men by lying and denying his master three times (Matt 26:69-75)*

1.3 Jesus: Bridegroom of the Church (faithful, submissive, pure wife): 2 Cor 11:2; Rev 12:1

"For I feel a divine jealousy for you, since I betrothed you to one husband, to present you as a pure virgin to Christ" 2 Cor 11:2

"And a great sign appeared in heaven: a woman clothed with the sun, with the moon under her feet, and on her head a crown of twelve stars" Rev 12:1

Explanations:

a. *What did John see in heaven?* **A woman** *"This woman represents God's Church of all ages*

b. *What was she clothed with?* **The sun**

"The sun represents Jesus and his righteousness. (Mal 4:2)"

c. *What was under her feet?* **The Moon**

"The moon only reflects sunlight. It represents the sacrificial system of the Old Testament, which only reflected the light that the Gospel has in Jesus."

d. *What did she have on her head?* **A crown**

"The crown of 12 stars represents the twelve apostles and their work (Matt 10:1-4)"

Summary: *The sun and moon forming a global whole symbolize the entire Church in history: The Church before the cross and the Church after the cross.*

The Bible illustrates the relationship of Jesus (bridegroom) with the bride (Church) through the relationship of husband and wife in marriage. Just as in human union, the bride must show fidelity and submission to her husband; the Church's responsibility toward Jesus is submission and faithfulness. An unfaithful and insubordinate Church is not Jesus's Church, and members who may be in it should question their affiliation with Jesus and his Church.

1.4 Jesus's Return and the Church: John 14:1-3

"Let not your hearts be troubled. Believe in God; believe also in me... I go to prepare a place for you, and if I go and prepare a place for you, I will come again and will take you to myself, that where I am you may be also"

- *By this declaration, Jesus affirms unequivocally that he is coming back for his Church. The signs being fulfilled each day say that this return is near. The concern of every Christian should be: preparation and vigilance, according to what is written in Matt 24:42, 44: "Therefore, stay awake, for you do not know on what day your Lord is coming... Therefore, you also must be ready, for the Son of Man is coming at an hour you do not expect"*

1.5 The characteristics of Jesus's Church: Rev 14:12; Rev 12:17; Rev 19:10

"Here is a call for the endurance of the saints, those who keep the commandments of God and their faith in Jesus" Rev 14:12

"Then the dragon became furious with the woman and went off to make war on the rest of her offspring, on those who keep the commandments of God and hold to the testimony of Jesus" Rev 12:17

"For the testimony of Jesus is the spirit of prophecy" Rev 19:10

The above passages reveal the characteristics of Jesus's Church:

1. The woman (Church) is engaged in a struggle with the dragon (Satan)
2. She is represented by a remnant (or residue)
3. She keeps God's commandments
4. She is devoted to the study of prophecy

Truth has never necessarily been on the side of the majority. In Noah's time, only eight (8) people were saved, because they alone believed. Every sincere person should, independently, test their religious beliefs against these criteria to determine whether or not they are part of Jesus's Church.

2. How to become part of Jesus's Church? Mark 16:16

"Whoever believes and is baptized will be saved, but whoever does not believe will be condemned"

- *Baptism is the entrance door to Jesus's Church. It is the means of publicly and solemnly expressing one's faith in Jesus's sacrifice. When one is convinced of the truth of the Gospel, there is no other decision to make than that of the Ethiopian Eunuch: "See, here is water! What prevents me from being baptized?" Acts 8:36*

RECAP: REFLECTION THEMES DRAWN FROM THIS STUDY

1. Fundamental difference between the Church of the New Testament and that of the Old?

2. Who is the foundation of the Church?

3. Indicate, according to Revelation, the characteristics of Jesus's Church

CHAPTER 12: THE ART OF MAKING DECISIONS

10.1 The Decision: Definition

A decision is the act of a person who, after being exposed to the Gospel (through a Bible study or a series of Bible conferences), freely chooses to apply the new truth they have received in their life. This choice is genuine and complete when it is made without any form of constraint or external pressure, meaning with the full autonomy of the individual's will.

It is thus understood that a true decision involves two (2) fundamental concepts: knowledge of the Word and free choice. These two elements must necessarily be present together. For example, a person who has been introduced to the science of salvation and the fundamental biblical doctrines certainly has knowledge of the Word. However, if that person is compelled to accept this truth due to the influence of a parent, friend, fiancé, spouse, etc., the decision is not considered perfect.

On the other hand, there are people who sincerely decide to join the Church for relatively trivial reasons, such as seeing a temple in a dream or being attracted to the lifestyle of a certain group of Christians. These people have not yet been introduced to Jesus, who is the way, the truth, and the life. In this case, while the choice is freely made, it remains fragile and is unlikely to withstand the test of time or the challenges of Christian life.

That being said, the best approach for a disciple of Jesus is first to encourage all those they encounter to study the Holy Scriptures and leave the rest to the work of the Holy Spirit. This approach avoids putting the cart before the horse.

10.2 The Form of the Decision

A decision is a public stance, an unequivocal act that reflects the will to abandon a former lifestyle and prior convictions to embrace new ones, deemed consistent with the newly acquired knowledge of the inspired text. This decision is both an end and a beginning. While it cannot be reduced to a mere transition from one religion to another, the change is often so radical — with new biblical truths that are sometimes opposed to previous experiences — that starting a new journey with God almost inevitably involves a shift in religious perspective.

A decision in spiritual matters always takes a concrete form and has nothing in common with mere intellectual or theoretical consent or acceptance.

10.3 Decision: Why?

The goal of every lay preacher or disciple should be to win souls for Christ; this is entirely legitimate. We should not set less ambitious goals, just as a farmer rightly expects the seed sown in the ground to produce fruit.

However, a preacher should never feel a sense of failure, disappointment, or bitterness when a person exposed to the Gospel does not make a decision. To do so is to assume God's role and claim a right that does not belong to us.

Our role as evangelists is like that of a farmer: we only sow the seed of the Gospel in people's hearts. It is solely the action of the Holy Spirit that causes it to germinate and mature. We are not granted the knowledge or understanding of the exact timing or mechanisms of a person's conversion.

People who, according to our human perception, were initially labeled as the most hostile to the Gospel have, in some cases, later revealed themselves to be fertile ground for God, souls thirsty for truth and love. Conversely, others whom we initially believed to be highly receptive to the message of the cross turned out to be less responsive.

10.4 Call to Decision

The call to decision is a direct invitation to accept a truth. This must be done at the most appropriate time, just as a ripe fruit needs to be harvested at the right moment. The following statement highlights the importance of this call:

"Many souls are in the valley of decision and need a clear and personal call to be made to them so that they may surrender and take their stand on the side of the Lord."— *Ellen G. White, Testimonies, Vol 1, p. 646*

10.5 Steps of the Call

The steps of the call to decision relate to the different types of calls. This is where the preacher must demonstrate great wisdom and tact. Acting too hastily can result in the loss of a soul that was willing to give themselves to the Lord. It would be very unwise to make a direct call to a decision during the first session of a series of Bible studies or public conferences.

In summary, there are two (2) main types or categories of calls:

10.5.1 Psychological Call

This call is generally made during the presentation of introductory or general topics. It often takes the form of simple questions for which it is almost certain that the response will be "yes." Participants are often invited to respond by raising their hands. Examples of such questions include:

- "Who believes that the Bible is inspired by God?"
- "I want to see the hands of those who would like to live with Jesus for all eternity."

These questions elicit positive responses. Through these questions, the preacher trains the audience to say "yes," meaning to agree with him.

10.5.2 Direct Call

This is a call that directly engages the participant's responsibility. A positive response to these questions is expected to significantly alter the individual's Christian behavior. For instance, an example of a direct call might be:

- "Are you willing to be baptized?"

The response to this call is expressed either through a decision card or by a public gesture such as raising a hand or standing up. Some preachers prefer to use decision cards because their discreet nature makes it easier for shy individuals to respond. Experience in missionary work has justified this method.

However, the decision card should be considered a preliminary step in the call. Those who fully and unreservedly decide to follow the Lord must later publicly express this decision.

10.6 The Limits of the Call

When presenting the Holy Word, the preacher must keep in mind that not all those invited will accept the call. This reality aligns with the message of Jesus. In this context, we should remember the following points:

1. The Gospel Must Be Preached as a Testimony

"This gospel of the kingdom will be preached in the whole world as a testimony to all nations, and then the end will come."— *Matthew 24:14*

"Son of man, I have made you a watchman for the house of Israel; so, hear the word I speak and give them warning from me... When I say to the wicked, 'You wicked person, you will surely die,' and you do not speak out to dissuade them from their ways, that wicked person will die for their sin, and I will hold you accountable for their blood. But if you do warn the wicked person to turn from their ways and they do not do so, they will die for their sin, though you will be saved."— *Ezekiel 33:7-9*

2. **Each Heart Represents a Type of Soil as in the Parable of the Sower. Matthew *13:4-7***

3. **In the Parable of the Invited Guests, Everyone Found Justifiable Excuses to Refuse the Invitation — *Luke 14:15-24***

10.7 Call and Excuses

In the parable of the guests (Luke 14:15-24), each person invited found a legitimate reason not to respond to the invitation. The same happens today. When God's Word is proclaimed, some sincere souls decide to conform to it, but others do not. The latter often present excuses to justify themselves.

Here are some of the most common excuses, along with the corresponding biblical responses:

1. **"Not now"**

Response: "For he says, 'In the time of my favor I heard you, and in the day of salvation I helped you.' I tell you, now is the time of God's favor, now is the day of salvation."2 *Corinthians 6:2*

"God again set a certain day, calling it 'Today.' This he did when a long time later he spoke through David, as in the passage already quoted: 'Today, if you hear his voice, do not harden your hearts.'" — *Hebrews 4:7*

2. **"My friends will make fun of me"**

Response: "If you belonged to the world, it would love you as its own. As it is, you do not belong to the world, but I have chosen you out of the world. That is why the world hates you."— *John 15:19*

3. **"My spouse, brothers, sisters, father, or mother will oppose me"**

Response: "A man's enemies will be the members of his household... Anyone who loves their father or mother more than me is not worthy of me; anyone who loves their son or daughter more than me is not worthy of me."— *Matthew 10:36-37*

4. "I can't leave my church"

Response: "Then I heard another voice from heaven say: 'Come out of her, my people so that you will not share in her sins so that you will not receive any of her plagues. ***"Revelation 18:4***

"I have other sheep that are not of this sheep pen. I must bring them also. They too will listen to my voice, and there shall be one flock and one shepherd."— *John 10:16*

5. "My pastor and friends warned me"

Response: "But Peter and John replied, 'Which is right in God's eyes: to listen to you or him? You be the judges!'"— *Acts 4:19*

6. "I am too great a sinner"

Response: "Come now, let us settle the matter,' says the Lord. 'Though your sins are like scarlet, they shall be as white as snow; though they are red as crimson, they shall be like wool.'"— *Isaiah 1:18*

"Here is a trustworthy saying that deserves full acceptance: Christ Jesus came into the world to save sinners—of whom I am the worst."— *1 Timothy 1:15*

7. "I can't give up certain things (pleasures, jewelry, etc.)"

Response: "Do not love the world or anything in the world. If anyone loves the world, love for the Father is not in them. For everything in the world—the lust of the flesh, the lust of the eyes, and the pride of life—comes not from the Father but from the world. The world and its desires pass away, but whoever does the will of God lives forever."— ***1 John 2:15-17***

8. "There are too many hypocrites in the church"

Response: "Jesus told them another parable: 'The kingdom of heaven is like a man who sowed good seed in his field. But while everyone was sleeping, his enemy came and sowed weeds among the wheat, and went away... Let both grow together until the harvest. At that time, I will tell the harvesters: First collect the weeds and tie them in bundles to be burned; then gather the wheat and bring it into my barn.'"
— *Matthew 13:24-30*

9. "I can't be baptized a second time"

Response: "Did you receive the Holy Spirit when you believed?" They answered, "We have not even heard that there is a Holy Spirit." So he asked, "Then what baptism did you receive?" "John's baptism," they replied. Paul said, "John's baptism was a baptism of repentance. He told the people to believe in the one coming after him, that is, in Jesus." On hearing this, they were baptized in the name of the Lord Jesus.
—*Acts 19:2-5*

CHAPTER 13: THE ART OF ANSWERING QUESTIONS

13.1 Importance of Questions

When delivering a message, whether during a Bible study or a series of biblical conferences, the preacher does not have the means to fully measure the level of understanding or assimilation of the message by the audience. While the audience's reactions (gestures, facial expressions) can provide some insight, they are not sufficient. It is mainly through the questions posed by the audience that one can gauge the impact of the message delivered. A preacher should never dismiss or consider the questions asked as unimportant.

13.2 Ways to Answer Questions

The approach to answering questions varies depending on whether it is a Bible study or lay preaching (biblical conferences).

13.2.1 Bible Study

While it is true that the student's questions are important, it is equally true that, from the outset, the rules of engagement must be established and made clear:

1. Questions should be asked at the end of the presentation —

Constant interruptions during the presentation would disrupt the flow of the study and cause the preacher to lose his train of thought.

2. Questions must be related to the subject being studied —

Questions that are not aligned with the topic being studied should be kindly postponed to be addressed at a later time. For example:

- General questions related to topics not included in the study plan.
- Questions related to planned topics that will be addressed later according to the order of the planned subjects.

13.2.2 Lay Preaching

For lay preaching (public conferences), it is not advisable to answer questions at the end of the session. Discussions between the preacher and participants at the end of the session could reduce or weaken the impact of the message in the minds of some attendees. It could also lead to confusion among the sincerest souls.

To avoid this, the preacher may set aside a special time for answering questions, either within the program (before the sermon) or on a specific day dedicated to this purpose.

Participants may also be invited to submit their questions in writing during the sessions, with answers provided on a designated day of the week chosen by the preacher. This approach allows the preacher time to properly prepare and document answers with relevant biblical references.

CHAPTER 14: EXEGESIS AND PREACHING

14.1 Exegesis: Definition and Content

The term **"Exegesis,"** derived from the Greek word *eksegesis* (meaning explanation, interpretation), signifies:

"Philological, historical, or doctrinal interpretation or explanation of a text that is obscure or subject to discussion."

While exegesis can be applied to other fields, such as philosophy and science, the type of exegesis that concerns us here is essentially biblical. It focuses on the interpretation or explanation of the sacred text, namely the Bible. This definition points us to three (3) key concepts: Philology, History, and Doctrine.

In light of this, the exegetical study of the biblical text is generally conducted from three perspectives: philological, historical, and doctrinal. We illustrate each of these concepts through examples from the Word of God.

1. Philological or Literary Aspect

Philology, from the Greek *philologia* (love of words, letters, literature), aims to restore the original content of texts known from multiple sources, that is, to select the most authentic text possible.

In this context, under the philological aspect of exegesis, theologians seek to understand the meaning of the original texts of the Bible (Hebrew or Greek) to comprehend and explain the modern translation of a text.

"When comparing different translations, we sometimes find different words for the same concept. Why? Because Hebrew and Greek words, like French words, have various meanings. Often, the different translations are complementary. We can use them in our message to better clarify the concept employed by the biblical author — for example, comparing it with a modern version where the words translated are rendered with terms closer to the true meaning of the original."

Here are two illustrative examples from the Word of God:

- **Example 1:** *"But I tell you that anyone who divorces his wife, except for sexual immorality, and marries another woman commits adultery." (Matthew 19:9)*

The question often asked about this text is:

"Does the 'infidelity' mentioned by Jesus here, in the context of marriage, also mean 'failure to fulfill mutual commitments made by the spouses'?"

An exegetical study of the term "infidelity," as rendered by Louis Segond, TOB, and BFC, reveals that the Greek word used in the original text is *porneia*, which means "sexual misconduct." The King James Version translates it as "sexual immorality." This means that the infidelity in question here, according to the original text, refers solely to sexuality and not to a symbolic or figurative approach (e.g., infidelity in the mutual commitments of spouses).

- **Example 2:***"For the husband is the head of the wife as Christ is the head of the church." (Ephesians 5:23, LSG)*

The word "head," as rendered by Louis Segond and certain other Bible translators, is the Greek term *kephalè* (meaning "head"). This implies that the man is the head of the woman, just as Christ is the head of the Church. This sheds important light on the meaning of the term "head" as God intends for man, distinct from other possible connotations or implications (e.g., tyrant, oppressor, etc.).

Exegesis, in this sense, is a matter for specialists (exegetes) who have access to the sources, unlike the ordinary theologian or preacher. Therefore, whenever we discuss exegesis here, we will not engage in in-depth exegesis but rather selective exegesis.

2. Historical and Cultural Aspects

From this perspective, exegesis focuses on placing texts within their historical and cultural contexts to understand them better.

Sometimes, a reader may encounter difficulties in discovering the meaning of a text due to linguistic, cultural, and temporal barriers.

"Before seeking to understand what the text may have to say to us, it is essential to first see what it had to say to its original audience or recipients." **(A.Kuen, Comment Prêcher et l'Art de Communiquer)**

According to A. Vinet: *"A text is drawn from the Word of God only when we give it the meaning intended by the sacred author."*

Wolfgang Klippert also asserts: *"What does the text have to say to me? This is a good question, but we ask it too soon. This text first had a specific meaning for those to whom it was originally addressed."*

This perspective requires bridging the gap between the past and the present. As S. Greidanus puts it: *"When transferring a message from the past to the present, the preacher must bridge the historical-cultural chasm that separates the world of the text from our contemporary world."*

Two biblical examples illustrate this historical-cultural aspect of exegesis:

- **Example 1**: *"As in all the churches of the saints, women should remain silent in the churches. They are not allowed to speak but must be in submission, as the law says. If they want to inquire about something, they should ask their husbands at home; for it is disgraceful for a woman to speak in the church."* (1 Corinthians 14:33-35)
- **Example 2**: *"A woman should learn in quietness and full submission. I do not permit a woman to teach or to assume authority over a man; she must be quiet."* (1 Timothy 2:11-12)

Do these two passages imply that women, for all time, are forbidden from speaking or teaching in church?

At this point, it is essential to understand the role of women in biblical history and, in particular, in the Church of Corinth. Historically, women played a subordinate role. During Israel's exodus from Egypt, God instructed Moses to conduct a census, counting only males (Numbers 1:2). Later, upon leaving the desert and before entering Canaan, another census was conducted under the same criteria (Numbers 26:4).

In the New Testament, when Jesus performed the miracles of feeding the multitudes, only the number of men present was recorded, excluding women and children (Matthew 14:21, 15:38).

On the other hand, at the time of the writing of this text from 1 Corinthians, among the Jews as well as among the Greeks, women had no public life, as they were absent from it, relegated to the background. They lived their lives as housewives with gentleness and discretion alongside their husbands and children. Taking into account the time and the socio-cultural situation of that era, and to avoid anything that could harm decency in Christian assemblies, Paul was therefore compelled to make this statement.

Based on this fact, if there were points that were not too clear for them in the assemblies, it was best for women to seek clarification from their husbands at home.

This statement from 1 Corinthians 14:33 also suggests a certain confusion within the Church of Corinth caused by the intervention of some women during a possible discussion. The protest of certain men, due to the aforementioned views of that time, made the apostle realize the need to establish safeguards to prevent any resurgence of such a situation. Therefore, it is in light of the customs of the time among the Jews and the Greeks that the aforementioned texts must be interpreted.

Moreover, it should also be noted that the term "speak" that the apostle uses in 1 Corinthians 14:34 (according to the original) is not "lego," which means "to speak, to reason," but "laleô," which means "to speak, to chat." Paul simply wanted to forbid any impropriety and indecency in Christian assemblies.

It is also within this same context that Paul's statement in 1 Timothy 2:11-12 should be understood, where he says, "I do not permit a woman to teach," since women, considered as minors, were excluded from religious life.

This is evidenced by the following excerpt: "*The woman in Hebrew society: In the Hebrew world, as in most of the Middle East, the woman occupied a completely subordinate position. Women were practically excluded from religious life, which was so important for the Hebrews. It was believed that women were not capable of receiving religious instruction...*

Women were excluded from the men's court. Their court was located five steps below that of the men. The same was true in synagogues: women were strictly separated, and often relegated to the back rows. Their presence did not count, whereas the presence of ten men was sufficient for the celebration of worship. Even minor men could read the Law and the Prophets, but women could not. This explains the disdain of rabbis for women: a rabbi could not address a woman in public. This exclusion of women was reflected in many prohibitions. They could neither speak in the synagogue nor testify in a trial (except in very rare cases), nor participate in meals when there were guests. In marriage, only the man could decide on a divorce: he simply had to write a letter of repudiation, without which the wife could not remarry."— **Les femmes, Dossiers libres, Paris, Ed du Cerf, 1980, pp. 12-14**

This is why, in summary, it is not possible to validly explain or interpret these instructions of Paul recorded in 1 Corinthians 14 and 1 Timothy 2 without placing them in their historical context.

Finally, it must be acknowledged that, for centuries and up to modern times, there has been a positive evolution in the role and status of women. Women have become acutely aware of this widespread historical and cultural contempt for women. They feel the need to bring to light the beauty, strength, dynamism, and diversity of women's experiences.

Here is the translation of the text as requested:

3. Doctrinal Aspect

It involves interpreting or explaining a text based on its context within a chapter, within a book, or its correlation with other books of the Bible.

For A. Pohl, placing the text back in its context *"is like plugging a lamp into an electrical circuit: the text is illuminated by its context."* It is necessary not only to place the text in its context but also to place it in the general context of the book. *"The book has a general introduction that is reflected in every text that is part of it. Hence, it is important to consult an introduction to the book specifying the author, recipients, circumstances of writing, occasion, and especially the purpose of the writing... However, this does not mean carrying out an in-depth exegesis of each biblical text, but rather a selective exegesis that primarily retains the essential ideas useful for the message that has been laid on our hearts."* — Alfred Kuen, Comment Prêcher ou l'Art de Communiquer l'Essentiel, p. 109

The following passages illustrate this aspect of exegesis.

Example (1): *"Let no one judge you in food or drink"* — **Colossians 2:16 (a)**

A superficial reading of this text leads opponents of the health regimen to claim that, contrary to the rules outlined in Leviticus 11, Paul is declaring here that there are no restrictions on eating and drinking.

The exegesis of this portion of the text, in its doctrinal aspect, requires placing it in its context to understand it, which means reading the preceding and following verses. This approach highlights the following points:

- **Verse 8:** "See to it that no one takes you captive through philosophy and empty deceit, according to human tradition, according to the elemental spirits of the world, and not according to Christ."
- **Verse 18:** "Let no one disqualify you, insisting on self-abasement and the worship of angels, dwelling on visions..."

- **Verse 20:** "If you have died with Christ to the elemental spirits of the world, why do you submit to regulations as though you still lived in the world?"
- **Verse 21:** "Do not handle! Do not taste! Do not touch!"

The analysis of these verses surrounding Colossians 2:16 shows that Paul is not addressing the health regimen (clean and unclean meats) as described in the Bible (Leviticus 11), but rather addressing cases of people who, through their philosophy, deceit, and reliance on human tradition and the elementary principles of the world, seek to impose on Christians certain practices or abstentions related to eating and drinking that are not by the precepts of God's Word.

Jewish leaders, in their religious practices, established a set of rules, principles, and traditions that had no scriptural basis. And Jesus never hesitated to reprimand them harshly: *"Thus you nullify the word of God for the sake of your tradition."* — (Matthew 15:6)

This automatically brings to mind the case of pagans or recently converted Jews who wanted to impose their former dietary practices on the Christians of Colossae after their conversion.

Using this same doctrinal approach to exegesis, one can also interpret the second part of Colossians 2:16, which refers to festivals and Sabbaths: *"Or about a festival, a new moon, or Sabbaths."*

In this case, as highlighted at the beginning of this chapter; to understand this portion of the text, it is necessary not only to place it within the context of the chapter (for example, verse 17) but also to refer to another book of the Bible (Leviticus 23) to establish the difference between the seventh-day Sabbath and ceremonial Sabbaths or festivals.

14.2 Exegesis and Meditation on the Text

If exegesis seeks to find the interpretation of a verse or passage from a philological, historical, and doctrinal perspective, this approach should not lead the preacher to get lost in purely intellectual and theoretical considerations. The purpose of preaching is not primarily to address the listener's mind but rather to touch their heart and soul. The purpose of preaching is to transform the listener's life — in other words, to save them.

The message must "land" to reach the individual in their intimate and personal life; otherwise, it would resemble more of a masterclass lecture by a professor at a Bible Seminary or a Faculty of Theology. The preacher would have spoken well but would not have preached.

According to A. Pohl: *"Exegesis without meditation leads to the slavery of words without penetration to the Word. Then, one only has stones instead of bread."*

On the other hand, he points out that the opposite is just as harmful, that is, meditation without exegesis: *"Meditation without exegesis, on the other hand, leads to the slavery of the self. One engages personally, but only opens to a superficially understood text and remains alone with one's thoughts. Nothing new is experienced. The text cannot say what it means. It only serves as a springboard for our preconceived thoughts. This is the origin of all pious and boring sermons."*— A. Pohl, 1979, p. 8

In short, it must be concluded that if exegesis without meditation leads to dry, superficial, and lifeless preaching, meditation without exegesis results in self-centered preaching that makes little use of biblical thought — the very essence of preaching, which is the act of communicating the Word of God.

CONCLUSIONS

Undoubtedly, you have learned many new concepts while reading this book. Perhaps this exercise has helped you recall or refresh knowledge you already had — knowledge related to techniques for missionary visits, Bible study, and preaching in general.

I would be remiss if I did not conclude this exciting journey with you by offering the following advice:

The ideas presented here are not one-size-fits-all solutions. No expert in homiletics or experienced evangelist has ever claimed that these techniques will necessarily produce the same results in every situation. We have already stated that preaching is, first and foremost, an art before it is a science — in other words, the art of skillfully combining the ingredients learned or known.

The preacher is much like a cook. When preparing a dish, if you give the same ingredients to several different chefs, you will end up with different dishes with distinct flavors because each chef's know-how and ingenuity come into play.

Preaching and evangelism are not exact sciences. They fall more under the domain of the human sciences — psychology, communication, and sociology. In short, the effectiveness of preaching inevitably depends on the personality of the preacher.

The purpose of preaching is to save souls. The techniques learned in universities or theological faculties may make you an excellent speaker capable of impressing an audience, but they do not necessarily make you a preacher. A preacher is someone who seeks to find the path to the heart to save souls.

No matter the topics addressed or the methods used to present them before an audience, the ultimate goal should be to touch and transform hearts.

Cultivate humility. The greatest quality of a preacher should be humility. Try, as much as possible, to step aside so that Jesus may be seen. Winning a soul does not depend on the techniques learned or applied but on the work of the Holy Spirit, who touches hearts and convinces them.

This humility should also drive you to seek the advice and criticism of more experienced people, either before or after delivering a message. The people around you (spouse, husband, children) should be your first and most honest critics.

Always aim for excellence. When you stand before an audience or even in an individual contact (such as a Bible study), you are representing the King of kings; this is an honor. This task should never be carried out with the slightest negligence. Strive for excellence! This goal will be achieved if you devote all the necessary attention to preparing your message. Take the time needed to prepare your message, as it is an unpardonable error to do otherwise.

Advance with patience. Do not expect to be an effective evangelist or preacher right from the start. All seasoned preachers have gone through phases of trial and error and experimentation. Do not be discouraged, and above all, do not measure your performance against the success of those who already have many years of experience.

Maturity and experience are acquired over time. Be an instrument in the hands of God, and never forget this thought: *"God does not call the qualified; rather, He qualifies those whom He calls."*

BIBLIOGRAPHY

Adams, J . *Pulpit Speech*, **Philadelphia Presbyterian & Ref**. Publ., 1972

Antomarchi, A . *Listening to the Spirit*, Privas, 1952

Beckam, William A *Redefining Revival: Biblical Patterns for Missions, Evangelism, and Growth*

Bohren, Rudolf . *Preaching the Preaching of Another*, in *Hokhma* No. 48 (1991)

Bonjour, Juan A . *The Bible Answers,* Inter-American Publishing House, Florida, USA, 1991

Bonhoeffer, D . *The Word of Preaching,* Geneva, Labor & Fides, 1992

Bosch, J . *Preaching Course*, Christian Training Center, Paris

Braga, James . *How to Prepare a Biblical Message*, Vida Publishing, Deerfield Florida (USA), 1987

Chappel, C. G . *Ten Rules for Living*, New York – Nashville, 1938

CGA *Missionary Training Manual,* Department of Lay Activities (French Edition) *Listening to the Bible*, Editions Vie et Santé, Dammarie-les - Lys, France, 2001

Dubois, J *Homiletics,* mimeographed course notes, n.d.

Evans, W. P *How to Prepare Sermons*, Chicago, Moody Press, 1964 (1913)

Ferrari, Lucius *Prompta Bibliotheca,* Venice, 1763

Flori, Jean & R. Henri *Creation and Evolution,* SDT Editions, Dammarie-les-Lys, France, 2001

Greidanus, S *The Modern Preacher and the Ancient Text (Interpreting and Preaching Biblical Literature)*, Grand Rapids: Eerdmans; Leicester: Inter-Varsity Press, 1988

Klippert, W *From Text to Sermon,* Wuppertal-Zurich, Brockhaus, 1995

Kuen, Alfred *How to Preach or the Art of Communicating the Essentials*, Emmaus Editions (Switzerland), 1998

Leflon, Jean *History of the Church from Its Origins to the Present*, 1949

Lenoir, Jean Raymond *Witnesses of the Present Truth*, SDT Editions, 1975

Perry, L. M – *Biblical Preaching for Today's World,* Moody Press, Chicago, 1973

Pohl, A *Guide to Preaching,* Wuppertal-Kassel, Oncken, 1979

Reymond, Bernard *With a Living Voice: Orality and Preaching*, Editions Labor et Fides, 1998

Stott, J *Between Two Worlds: The Art of Preaching in the Twentieth Century*, Grand Rapids: Eerdmans, 1982

Vanoye, Francis *Expression and Communication*, Colin, Paris, 1990

Vinet, A *Homiletics or the Theory of Preaching,* Paris, 1873

Vivarès, Patrice *The Call of the Word: An Essay on Preaching*, Soceval Editions, 2000

White, Ellen G – *Gospel Ministry*, SDT Editions, Dammarie-les-Lys (S & M), 1951

The Great Controversy, Inter-American Edition, 2012

Evangelism, Editions Vie et Santé, 2000

The Ministry of Healing, Pacific Press Publishing Association, 1977

Youte, Vaillant *Reflections on Homiletics, Preaching, and Evangelism,* Seventh-day Adventist Federation of Quebec, 2019-2020

www.ingramcontent.com/pod-product-compliance
Lightning Source LLC
Chambersburg PA
CBHW051145120626
46547CB00012B/953